THE AZTECS

LOST CIVILIZATIONS

The books in this series explore the rise and fall of the great civilizations and peoples of the ancient world. Each book considers not only their history but their art, culture and lasting legacy and asks why they remain important and relevant in our world today.

Already published:

The Aztecs Frances F. Berdan
The Barbarians Peter Bogucki
Egypt Christina Riggs
The Etruscans Lucy Shipley
The Goths David M. Gwynn
The Greeks Philip Matyszak
The Indus Andrew Robinson
The Persians Geoffrey Parker and Brenda Parker
The Sumerians Paul Collins

THE
AZTECS
LOST CIVILIZATIONS

FRANCES F. BERDAN

REAKTION BOOKS

Published by Reaktion Books Ltd
Unit 32, Waterside
44–48 Wharf Road
London N1 7UX, UK

www.reaktionbooks.co.uk

First published 2021
Copyright © Frances F. Berdan 2021

Printed and bound in India by Replika Press Pvt. Ltd

A catalogue record for this book is available from the British Library

ISBN 978 1 78914 360 7

CHRONOLOGY

c. AD 1–650	Dominance of Teotihuacan
c. 950–1175	Dominance of Tula
1150–1350	Migrations of *Chichimeca* into central Mexico
1325	Founding of Tenochtitlan
1428–30	Formation of the Aztec Triple Alliance
Early 1450s	Devastating famine in central Mexico, especially the Basin of Mexico
1465	Chalco conquered, facilitating trade routes to the east and south
1473	Tlatelolco conquered by Tenochtitlan
1479	Devastating defeat at the hands of the Tarascans
1487	Completion of a major expansion of the Great Temple of Tenochtitlan
1502	Motecuhzoma Xocoyotzin succeeds Ahuitzotl as Mexica king

1504, 1515	Notable wars between the Triple Alliance and Tlaxcalla and its allies
1519	Arrival of Spaniards under Cortés near present-day Veracruz
1519: 8 November	Meeting between Motecuhzoma and Cortés at the entrance to Tenochtitlan
1520: early July	'Noche Triste' or 'The Night the Spaniards Died at the Tolteca Canal'
1521: 13 August	Capture of Mexica king Cuauhtemoc by Spaniards

Volcanic stone sculpture of a man carrying a cacao pod, 1440–1521.

INTRODUCTION

The Aztecs were the last of a long succession of great civilizations that developed throughout the many and diverse regions of ancient Mesoamerica. In 1521 they were conquered by Spanish conquistadores and their numerous indigenous allies: at that point the Aztec empire and civilization became, on the surface, 'lost'. Their great capital city was demolished, their state institutions dismantled, their empire dissolved, and their theatrical religious ceremonies superseded by Christian ones. In this sense the Aztecs easily qualify as a fitting subject in this series of Lost Civilizations. But this is only part of the story. The empire may have been lost, but it has not disappeared from view. It is still discoverable.

Written Documents, Archaeology and Ethnography

The Aztecs were literate and amassed enormous libraries. Their pictorial books (codices) were produced by professional scribes and encompassed records as diverse as maps, dynastic and other histories, censuses, financial accounts, calendars, ritual almanacs and cosmological descriptions. Unfortunately, almost all of these books fell victim to the ravages of the conquest and its aftermath. Native books were considered by Spanish ecclesiastics to be 'books of the Devil' and were intentionally and systematically destroyed. However, a few survived and numerous other codices were produced in the early decades after the conquest, executed by native hands at the behest of either indigenous communities or Spanish

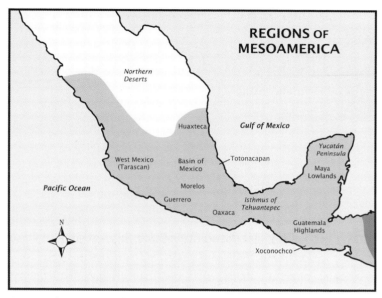

Regions of Mesoamerica during the Late Postclassic era.

political and religious overlords. These documents, if carefully filtered for Spanish influences, reveal rich nuggets of information on pre-Spanish Aztec life.

Sixteenth-century Spaniards were great fans of the written word and enthusiastically composed a wide variety of fascinating narratives. The conquistadores themselves wrote letters and other accounts describing their early encounters with the native peoples they would later conquer. These include the five letters of Hernando Cortés to the king of Spain, a 'true' history written by one of his soldiers, and several shorter but enlightening eyewitness accounts of the conquest itself. In the years following the conquest, Spanish religious persons such as the Dominican friar Diego Durán and the Franciscan friar Bernardino de Sahagún composed lengthy accounts of Aztec history and culture. Much can be believed in these and related accounts: Durán and others mention pictorial codices among their sources, Sahagún worked directly with knowledgeable native men in producing his encyclopaedic *Florentine Codex*, and native chroniclers such as Fernando Alva de Ixtlilxochitl also relied on pre-Spanish pictorial sources, now lost. And there is more: the Spaniards undertook censuses of native communities under their new colonial rule, produced a wide range of official reports, and inscribed innumerable tax and legal records.

The native people were neither idle nor passive in the face of this avalanche of Spanish documents. Some learned the alphabetic script early on, and produced for themselves and others great quantities of documents including wills, law suits, land claims, complaints and even letters, all in the native Nahuatl language. The language was tenacious: indigenous oral histories augmented by codices were written down in alphabetic script in Nahuatl, so today we have access to chronicles, histories, poetry, songs and sage advice from elders to help us reconstruct details of daily life in the ancient Aztec world.

Despite the richness and abundance of the documentary record, it is invariably flawed. For example, Cortés's letters were self-serving and the accounts of other Spanish conquistadores furthered their own personal goals and were grounded in their own cultural preconceptions. Spanish ecclesiastics avidly bent on conversion to Christianity expectedly denigrated native religious beliefs and ceremonies. In another vein, point of view often muddied the written word: for instance, a native noble recounting a pre-Spanish history wrote not only from the perspective of his elevated status but from that of his own particular city. Perspectives may be tied to factors such as social status, residence, ethnicity or occupational group, so intentional or unconscious biases seeped into the written record. Still, we rely heavily on early colonial written sources to look backward and reconstruct pre-Spanish Aztec life; the exercise requires teasing out pre-Columbian realities from colonial influences and transformations. And while documentary sources can be truly enlightening, they do not provide a complete picture of this 'lost civilization'. Many areas of life, such as women's activities and the daily lives of slaves, appear only as fleeting glimpses.

Archaeology offsets some of these shortcomings. Archaeological investigations uncover and interpret the material and physical remains of people who lived in the past. The Aztecs fortunately left behind many and myriad traces of their public and private lives. Archaeological evidence (some of it magnificent and sensational) derives from stationary constructions, portable objects and human biological remains. The Aztecs were builders on a grand scale, and left behind constructions including lofty temples, vast palaces, ballcourts, sweatbaths, skull racks, warrior assembly rooms, shrines, altars, schools, walls, pavements, dams, terraces, everyday houses and a large number of ritual caches. The grandest of these (especially temples and other symbols of Aztec religious and political primacy) were demolished during or shortly after the Spanish conquest, and other structures have been reduced to platforms and foundations over the centuries.

Spectacular Aztec objects have been widely known for centuries. During and shortly after the Spanish conquest, conquistadores (including Cortés) sent crates and crates of luxurious booty across the Atlantic to Spanish institutions and individuals (including the king, of course). Some of the earliest shipments were displayed at the king's court and later in the Hôtel de Ville of Brussels in 1520. There, after viewing great discs of gold and silver, two rooms full of native armour and weapons, and 'very strange' clothing and other wondrous objects, the renowned and keen-eyed painter Albrecht Dürer raved on and on that 'All the days of my life I have seen nothing that so rejoiced my heart as these things, . . . and I marveled at the subtle intellects of men in foreign parts.'[1] The Aztecs came to exemplify 'the exotic' in the minds of Europeans on the basis of these and other exotic objects, in tandem with reports from conquistadores, Spanish colonial administrators, and Christian friars and priests.

Interest in Aztec archaeological remains essentially lay dormant for most of the seventeenth and eighteenth centuries. This lull was interrupted in 1790 by the unearthing of two monumental Aztec stone sculptures in downtown Mexico City: the round 'Sun Stone' or 'Calendar Stone' (diam. 3.6 m/11.75 ft) and the statue of the mother goddess Coatlicue (h. 2.7 m/8.9 ft). The massive Tizoc Stone was uncovered the following year. Like many archaeological discoveries, these three were not intentionally excavated, but rather accidentally discovered, in this case by workers re-paving and installing drains in the city's main plaza (*zócalo*). Each of these monuments experienced idiosyncratic archaeological histories. For instance, when the Calendar Stone was discovered it was pulled into a vertical position so it could be easily studied, and on 2 July 1791 it was moved to the nearby cathedral and set prominently into that building's southwest tower. Suffering a great deal of wear and tear from this exposure, in 1885 the monument was moved to the city's early Museo Nacional. In 1964 it was transferred to its final destination, the Museo Nacional de Antropología in Chapultepec Park, where it can be seen today. Spanish suppression of the native religion led monks to bury the Coatlicue statue in the city's university courtyard; in 1803 the Prussian naturalist Alexander von Humboldt had it exhumed in order to examine it. The monks promptly reburied it after he left. Later, it also became a featured monument in Chapultepec Park's Museo Nacional.

Enthusiasm for the Aztecs was re-ignited with these spectacular discoveries. The nineteenth and early twentieth centuries saw the publication of these monuments (stimulating interest in Aztec archaeology), the founding of the Museo Nacional de Antropología (in 1825), and the initiation of significant archaeological investigations, primarily centred on Tenochtitlan, beneath today's downtown Mexico City. In 1914 archaeological investigations uncovered a corner of the Aztecs' Great Temple along with many ritual objects. There was no follow-up to this important discovery until 1978, when excavations of this greatest of all Aztec temples began in earnest.

The large-scale Basin of Mexico settlement pattern survey project initiated in 1960 opened up an entirely new approach to understanding the Aztec civilization. These eye-opening archaeological surveys revealed a landscape crowded with different types of settlement, shifting interest from the great urban centres to non-urban sites.[2] The many projects deriving from these surveys fed into problem-oriented archaeological research that had emerged in the mid-twentieth century and continues to the present day. These investigations have allowed archaeologists to refine chronologies and historical timelines, and to pursue topics such as population size, relationships among urban and rural settlements, political and social complexity, craft activities, trade and markets, and life at the household level. Archaeologists have also turned their attention to long-term cultural and political changes, and to the impact of the empire on its conquered regions. Using sophisticated twenty-first-century technologies, archaeologists can demonstrate how a master artisan fashioned a complicated feather headdress, recreate the origins and exchange routes of different types of pottery or stone objects, and unravel the meanings of thousands of artefacts buried in ritual caches. The list goes on and on, and in modern Aztec archaeology every new answer prompts another thought-provoking question.

Today, excavations and surveys of urban and rural sites have yielded a wealth of information on Aztec life, and we will meet up with several of these investigations throughout this book. The most significant of these are the long-term excavations in the heart of Mexico City at and around the Aztec Great Temple. But much archaeological research has also been undertaken in almost every corner of the Aztec empire. In addition to uncovering permanent structures, these excavations have also unearthed great quantities of portable artefacts. These range from monumental structures as grandiose as the Coyolxauhqui Stone (diam. 3.2 m/10.5 ft) found at the base of Tenochtitlan's Great Temple, to artefacts as small and delicate as a 10-centimetre (4 in.) alabaster deer, a diminutive jadeite bead, an obsidian blade, or delicate ear spools and lip plugs.

For archaeological purposes, artefacts are most useful when found *in situ* and recovered from the original site of their deposition (whether left behind intentionally or not). They can be evaluated in both time and space, and understood in the bigger picture of, say, a house, a temple or a community. There are, however, a great many artefacts housed in museums around the world, some of them unbelievably exquisite, and without any known or verifiable provenance. This does not mean they are useless: a fine turquoise stone mosaic, for instance, can be mined for its abundance of technological and symbolic information, such as the types of materials and their origins, the processes and sequences of construction, the probable tools used and the iconography and its meaning. And some delicate artefacts, such as the feather shield and headdress currently housed in Vienna, are manufactured of perishable materials only rarely found in archaeological excavations, and their constructions have been meticulously studied.[3]

Human biological remains reveal much about the people themselves. They typically are found as burials or offerings; for instance, some human remains around Tenochtitlan's Great Temple consist of cremated remains of aristocrats, others are beheaded sacrificial offerings, and still others are the remains of children sacrificed to the rain god. Blood residue discovered in a nearby building points to ritual blood-letting. Elsewhere, some unearthed skulls have perforations at their temples, indicating that they were displayed on a skull rack. Taken together, human remains yield important information ranging from age and gender to medical conditions, possible occupations, migratory movements and manner of death.

The archaeological record augments and amplifies the documentary record in important ways and is constantly unfolding. As you read this, excavations in downtown Mexico City are uncovering evidence of ancient Aztec ritual activities, and research in other parts of the ancient empire is disclosing intriguing information, from the mundane to the sacred. A particular advantage of archaeology is that it does not suffer the special interests associated with written documents. That is, a royal palace was built in its time to convey wealth and power, but once abandoned its remains would later be found much as they were left behind (beyond destruction and looting). A burial was intentional, but the body and its grave goods were not laid out in a manner to deceive or impress some future archaeologist. Archaeological investigations also offer greater time depth than the documentary record, and with its focus on material remains, archaeology delves into aspects of life (such as house construction, craft techniques, diet and standards of living) often unavailable in the documents. Still, information gathered through excavation, survey or other archaeological techniques is inevitably incomplete and uneven. Following the conquest, the Spaniards intentionally built directly atop many of the existing Aztec cities and towns, using cut stone from Aztec structures in their own new buildings. Gaining access to an ancient site can be a major challenge. Archaeological information is also necessarily selective: artefacts made of perishable materials such as wood, cloth or feathers have survived only in exceptional contexts, and the recoverable material record usually only obliquely addresses abstract matters such as language, religious beliefs and social obligations.

Some of these shortcomings in the documentary and archaeological records are alleviated by recourse to modern ethnography. Today more than 2 million people speak Nahuatl, the Aztec language, which has remained remarkably tenacious despite five hundred years of Spanish and Mexican contact and culture change. Languages are robust reservoirs of a people's culture; they can reveal the subtle meanings of metaphors, the structure of family relations, and details ranging from farming to weaving to curing. Documents and archaeology normally fall short in these spheres of life. Beyond language, present-day descendants of Aztecs and other native groups continue some practices and customs based on ancient traditions: these range from the practicalities of farming and cooking to the more nuanced worlds of private and communal rituals. Decades of ethnographic research have yielded more than a glimmer of Aztec daily lives that have persisted, with expected modifications, over nearly five centuries.

This book draws on all these lines of evidence, privileging no one source. In fact, our quest for an accurate reconstruction of this culture gains strength from relying on as many different sources as possible. In the chapters that follow, we will be digging deeper into these tantalizing sources as they reveal the ancient, 'lost' Aztecs, for the sources themselves are part of the cultures that fostered them.

A Few Essential Terms

As a final matter in this Introduction, I wish to clarify some slippery terminologies. The most problematic of these is the very title of this book, *Aztecs*. Here, this term refers to the Nahuatl-speaking people living in the Basin of Mexico during the Late Postclassic period (AD 1350–1521). The *Aztec empire* refers specifically to the empire built by the city-states of Tenochtitlan, Texcoco and Tlacopan, all in the Basin of Mexico. Creating some confusion, the term *Aztec* also refers to specific chronological periods, and to imperial artistic and architectural styles. Even more confounding is the frequent equivalence of *Aztec* with *Mexica*. This latter term specifically identifies the inhabitants of Tenochtitlan and its neighbouring city, Tlatelolco. People in Aztec-period central Mexico were often identified by their city or city-state of residence, so the *Mexica* were also called Tenochca or Culhua-Mexica. A final term of interest is *Mesoamerica*, a culture area encompassing the areas of Mexico and Central America that experienced the rise and fall of complex states and civilizations in pre-Columbian times.

And now, armed with these sources and terms, I wish to take you on a journey into the past. It is a past that is at the same time familiar and exotic – familiar because these were human beings doing very human things; exotic because some of those things may fall outside of your customary experience and you may find them singularly strange, perhaps even jarring. We will start in AD 1519.

ONE
'AN ENCHANTED VISION'

When we saw so many cities and villages built in
the water and other great towns on dry land and that
straight and level Causeway going towards Mexico, we
were amazed and said that it was like the enchantments
they tell of in the legend of Amadis, on account of the
great towers and cues [temples] and buildings rising from
the water, and all built of masonry. And some of our
soldiers even asked whether the things that we saw
were not a dream.[1]

With these words the Spanish conquistador Bernal Díaz
del Castillo recalled his first eye-opening view of the
great Aztec city of Tenochtitlan and its wondrous sur-
roundings. This foot soldier had come to the West Indies from
Spain in 1514 when he was about nineteen years old, and joined
Hernando Cortés's forces in Cuba in 1519.[2] After landing on the
Mexican coast near present-day Veracruz in April of that year, this
military contingent worked its way inland, in and out of Aztec
imperial boundaries, months later to arrive at the vast urban
expanse of the Basin of Mexico. They were spellbound as the gleaming panorama unfolded before them. What were they thinking?
What were they feeling? They had never seen anything quite like
this, but necessarily based their impressions on their own world
view. Where did that come from? What vision of the world did they
carry with them as they walked straight into this astonishing and
unfamiliar land?

Bernal Díaz and his Spanish colleagues were steeped in medieval and early modern Spanish traditions.[3] These included their

own recent history of conflicts between Spaniards and Moors that fostered aspirations of military valour, expectations of political loyalty, ideals of chivalry and honour, and a firm devotion to Christianity. These strongly grounded historical traditions were augmented by mythical or semi-mythical sagas of adventure and knightly courage. Among the most popular of these were the enthralling tales of Amadis of Gaul (reminiscent of the stories of King Arthur), brought to mind by Bernal Díaz as he gaped at the Aztec capital city. These romantic tales of derring-do follow the exploits of the seemingly invincible knight Amadis as he travels hither and thither about the countryside, enthusiastically vanquishing defiant enemies and conquering glorious cities. The Amadis tales speak often of beautiful towers, impregnable fortresses, elegant palace rooms and courtyards, and sweeping landscapes. One particular 'Amadis moment' may have popped into this foot soldier's mind as he gazed upon Tenochtitlan:

> and on the fifth day they found themselves near a very strong castle that overlooked salt water, and the castle was called Bradoyd, and it was the most beautiful in all that land, and was located on a high cliff, and on one side flowed that water and on the other there was a great marsh; and on the water side one could enter only by boat, and on the side toward the marsh there was a causeway so wide that one cart could go and another come, but at the entrance to the causeway there was a narrow bridge and it was a drawbridge.[4]

In November 1519 Bernal Díaz seems to have envisioned himself in such a setting, even though he wrote and rewrote his recollections from the 1550s until his death in 1584, many years after the events and personal experiences he describes in such colourful detail. And he sounds right out of the tales of Amadis when he states that one of his major goals in writing his account was to 'extol the adventures which we met with and the heroic deeds we accomplished during the conquest of New Spain and its provinces'.[5] These romantic ideals were offset by intense religious beliefs and practical aspirations of wealth in portable goods (especially gold) and control over new lands and labour to work those lands. Clearly the conquistadores were highly motivated and brought with them a constellation of preconceptions and ambitions as they entered this challenging and exotic land.

The 1524 Nuremberg Map of Tenochtitlan

Within a year Bernal Díaz's 'enchanted vision' was laid out in a map that encompassed the plan of Tenochtitlan and its surrounding lacustrine and urban landscape. The conquistadores entered this land along the southern causeway (on the left side of the map), having spent the night before in the lakeside city of Ixtapalapa (labelled Iztapalapa). Envision the Spaniards and the native allies they had collected along their journey from the coast, warily riding and walking along the broad causeway, passing multitudes of gawking people in canoes. They persevered step after step past flat-roofed houses and lofty temples, into the mysterious depths of the greatest city of the Aztec known world.

This renowned map was reportedly sent by Cortés with his second letter to the king of Spain in October 1520, almost ten months before the actual fall of the city to the Spaniards and their native allies. The map saw the light of day in Nuremberg in 1524 when it was published as a woodcut, created by a European craftsman and accompanying a Latin publication of Cortés's sensational second letter. It was designed to appeal and relate to a European audience, hence the medieval-looking towers, domes and spires; the alphabetic glosses; a wicker dyke; houses drawn in perspective (a style not used in pre-Spanish Aztec art); a Classical-style sculpture; two lions among the native zoo animals; a small cross attached to the great temple; and a prominent Habsburg flag. In this colour version of the map, the roofs of the houses are red-tiled. Overall the map depicts an orderly urban world, one that a European viewer would understand as 'civilized'. But 'civilized' is juxtaposed with 'barbaric' with the inclusion of manifestations of human sacrifice: a decapitated sculpture and two ominous-looking skull racks are conspicuous in the very heart of the city. Familiar but exotic – a publisher's dream.

There are convincing indications that the original prototype map was composed by an Aztec scribe. The map is schematic and focuses on balance and symmetry (native preoccupations), with no particular attention to distances or scale. In actuality, the city did not sit in the middle of the lake. Yet the map clearly features the city as central and dominant: it is shown as the *axis mundi*, as the Aztecs truly conceived it. It was the very centre of their conceptual terrestrial and cosmic world, and it makes sense that the map depicts all roads leading to the centre of this city, and particularly to its monumental temple. The precise alignment of the great temple and the division of the city into quarters are characteristically indigenous and all-important to their conception of their place in the natural and supernatural universe. Also, there are features in the map that are unlikely to have been observed or understood by the Spaniards. For instance, the sun appears in the gap between the main twin temples, perfectly poised as it would have been observed by the Aztecs during its rising at the equinoxes. And details such as the exact locations of the great Tlatelolco market (labelled 'Foru[m]'), the spring to the west that served as the source of their aqueduct, and the prominent dyke on the eastern side of the lake all appear in their proper places but were not

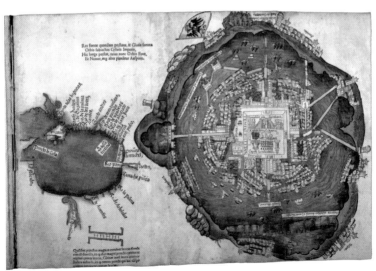

The 1524 Nuremberg Map of Tenochtitlan.

located in Cortés's second letter. Finally, west is at the top of the map, corresponding to other indigenous and indigenous-style maps from sixteenth-century central Mexico. With all of this in mind, the best-supported conclusion is that the German craftsman who created the woodcut worked from an indigenous prototype, embellishing it with his familiar buildings and other European features.[6]

This one map weaves together indigenous and European ideas and depictions of geographic space. It is an Aztec conception redesigned to suit European precepts and stylistic understandings. The map is a hybrid, an intricate blend. It provides a good starting-point to pursue a broad overview of landscapes, cities and towns, and the native people encountered by the Spaniards. But it is just one side of the story; as much as possible, the remainder of this book focuses on Aztec culture from the vantage point of the Aztecs themselves.

Landscapes

The lands that the Spanish conquistadores encountered on their trek from the Gulf Coast to highland Tenochtitlan were diverse and expansive: sand dunes and a broad coastal plain gave way to low-lying humid and semi-humid hills and then to more impressive mountains and deep *barrancas* (gorges), and on to dry stretches and broad, heavily populated plateaus. During their audacious journey the Spaniards experienced something of a microcosm of the Aztec imperial domain. They traversed hot tropical lowlands, encountered small communities nestled in the niches of verdant hillsides, marched more forthrightly across broad plains, weathered the travails of snowy mountain passes (even in August), and finally cast their eyes on the lake-dominated Basin of Mexico. While much of this was unfamiliar to the Spaniards, enough of it reminded them of their Spanish homeland in 'mountains, valleys and fields' and 'fertility, size and the cold, as well as in many other things' to prompt Cortés himself to suggest naming it New Spain.[7] The Spaniards were cognizant of the locations of cities, fortifications and numbers of native warriors, for their immediate needs and survival. They also took notice of particular Spanish interests in the new land, such as sources of water, timber, ores and agricultural crops, in thoughts of a future occupation.

The Spaniards had travelled in and out of the eastern Aztec empire, but similar ecologies were mirrored throughout the Aztec domain to the north, west and south. In their trek, mostly during the summer rainy season, the Spaniards essentially described individual microenvironments (although not calling them that) without the benefit of seeing the broader environmental sweep. Looking at the big picture today, the area encompassed by the Aztec empire lay entirely within the tropics. Variations in ecologies were determined primarily by elevation and rainfall, both of which differed regionally and seasonally. Modern geographers divide this complex world into three distinct zones: *tierra caliente, tierra templada* and *tierra fría*. The hub of the Aztec empire lay in *tierra fría*.

Tierra caliente (hot land) encompasses coastal plains and low-lying inland hills and flatlands, from sea level to an elevation of 1,000 metres (3,280 ft). These lands are hot and humid and typically experience high rainfall, all of which result in environments full of abundant wildlife, lush tropical vegetation and plentiful crop yields (often two harvests of staple crops yearly). In Aztec times, these were (and continue to be) lands of prowling jaguars, screeching monkeys, elegant birds of brilliant plumage, and prolific riverine and marine life. The Aztecs valued these lands as sources for prized goods and commodities such as cacao, cotton, greenstones, colourful feathers and fine salt. In the latter years of the empire, Aztec rulers conquered many cities in this zone, reaping precious tributes to enhance their own power and livelihoods.

Tierra templada (temperate land) lay between 1,000 and 2,000 metres (6,560 ft) in elevation. Here are found landscapes ranging from rugged mountain terrain to more gentle hills to vast river valleys. Seasonal (May–October) rainfall is uneven in this zone, resulting in microenvironments varying from dry scrublands to semi-humid hills to expansive grasslands to mountain forests. Aztec imperial control over temperate lands extended mostly to the south, east and west of their heartland in the Basin of Mexico, and provided the empire with fairly reliable stores of staple crops

Maize field in a highland landscape.

(especially maize and beans) and a miscellany of resources including turquoise stones, gold, copper, pigments and dyes, and bees' honey.

Tierra fría (cold land) lies above 2,000 metres and encompasses highland plateaus, lake-dominated basins and majestic volcanic mountains. Native vegetation responds to the high altitude and somewhat undependable rainfall: flat grasslands, vast farmlands, scrub woodlands and pine-oak forests are all found in this zone. Seasonal rainfall is more unpredictable than at lower elevations, and farmers always faced a relatively short growing season and the danger of devastating frosts. Yet in Aztec times this zone was a noted breadbasket, the conquistadores marvelling at almost endless stretches of cultivated fields on the highland plateaus. Deer and rabbits were common, millions of migratory birds descended on the lakes in annual swarms, and abundant aquatic resources attracted people for thousands of years prior to and during Aztec ascendency. The Aztecs themselves lived in *tierra fría*, and extracted resources such as timber, reeds, obsidian and salt from their own heartland and from nearby conquered regions.

The highland Basin of Mexico, sitting at 2,236 metres (7,379 ft) in elevation at its lowest point and therefore in *tierra fría*, was the heart of the Aztec empire. It encompasses approximately 7,000 square kilometres (2,700 sq. mi.). It is a basin by virtue of its system of interior drainage: it is surrounded by lofty mountains as high as 5,465 metres (18,035 ft) that spill rainfall into the lakes, with no outlet.[8] Flooding is (and was) a summer expectation. The empire's three capital cities, Tenochtitlan, Texcoco and Tlacopan (and a host of other smaller cities making the lake a densely populated urban complex), were established in and around a network of five lakes connected in varying degrees depending on wet or dry seasons. The southern and northern lakes are fresh and spring-fed. The eastern portion of the larger and lower Lake Texcoco is saline and unsuitable for agriculture (but was a productive setting for salt-making). In Aztec times the freshwater lakes and lake shores to

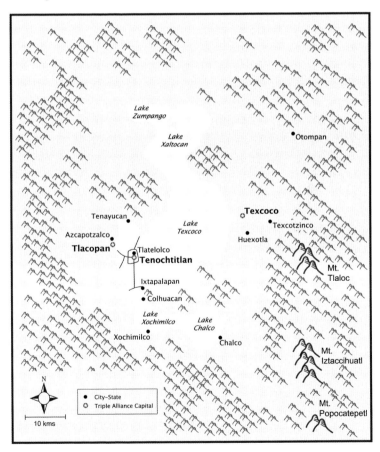

Map of the Basin of Mexico in 1519.

the south, west and north were intensively exploited for agriculture by the construction of swathes of land extending into them, a highly productive system called *chinampas*.

Vast armies of conquest radiated from the imperial Basin of Mexico cities. When they were successful, enormous quantities of tribute were regularly sent from conquered peoples, near and far, living in all three geographic zones. At the time of the Spanish arrival, the empire embraced approximately 200,000 square kilometres (77,220 sq. mi.). In 1519 the Aztec emperor and his two imperial colleagues held as many as four hundred city-states under their sway. Some of these (tributary provinces) were held under tight control while others (strategic provinces) were treated more as unequal allies, or client states. The central focus of all these polities, including Tenochtitlan itself, was a city or town and its adjacent or nearby territories. It was the grandest of these that impressed the Spaniards as they looked upon the glittering Basin of Mexico cities on that fateful day in November 1519.

Cities and Towns

As he marched to Tenochtitlan, Hernando Cortés observed the highland valleys and plateaus as crowded with cities, towns and villages, filled in between with fields upon fields of cultivated maize and beans. These political entities (city-states or *altepetl*) were the essential political and settlement units among the native people. An *altepetl* usually had one major population centre containing the primary temple, palace and market for the entirety of the polity, including attached towns and rural areas. It also enjoyed prominence as the home of the city-state's dynastic ruler. Spaniards cast these nucleated entities as cities and towns, and after the conquest they typically built Spanish-style settlements on top of these existing native communities.

Sixteenth-century Spaniards valued urban life: in Spain, they preferred living in cities and they carried over that priority to New Spain, gravitating to cities when possible. Initially they must have been at least somewhat relieved to encounter so many large and 'civilized' areas (although soon dismayed by the enormous numbers of warriors those cities contained). While still on the coast, the Spaniards founded the town of Villa Rica de la Veracruz and Bernal Díaz related that 'we laid out plans of a church, marketplace, arsenals, and all those things that are needed for a town.'[9] Spanish cities and towns also contained plazas and government buildings (including palaces), the whole usually laid out in neat grid patterns. Cortés often compared native cities he encountered to cities in Spain such as Seville, Cordova and Granada, and the similarities between Spanish and native cities is striking. Temples, plazas, marketplaces and palaces (embracing administrative offices) all characterized the typical central Mexican city encountered by the Spaniards. Tenochtitlan's layout resembled a grid structure, although this arrangement was rarely found in Mesoamerica. The finer points of architecture and urban adornments differed, but the basic elements of urban layout and content were recognizable, if exotic in details, to the Spaniards.

Their 'exotic' baseline was their history with the Moors; they cast their encounters with the Mesoamerican natives in terms of their known Moorish encounters.[10] Moorish terms for temples ('mosque' and *mezquita*) were often applied to native temples by Spanish observers and chroniclers, and *mezquita* is written on the 1524 Nuremberg Map described at the outset of this chapter. Indeed, in 1541 an anonymous Spaniard (probably a cleric) apologized for his use of the term *mezquita* for *templo* in his annotations of a pictorial codex intended for the king of Spain.[11] Still, he did use that Moorish term, suggesting the degree to which nearly eight centuries of Moorish occupation of the Iberian Peninsula ingrained borrowed terminologies into Spanish, and the degree to which the Spaniards viewed the Aztecs as 'the other'.

People

We have no contemporaneous illustrations of individual Aztecs, beyond the generic images found in codices and on sculptures. We also have few textual descriptions of their physical appearance and manner. Among them is a brief general characterization by the enigmatically named Anonymous Conqueror: the people are 'well proportioned, tending to be tall rather than short; they are swarthy or brownish, of good features and mien. For the most part they are very skillful, stalwart and tireless.'[12]

A little more detail is provided by the conquistador Bernal Díaz del Castillo, who spent some time in the company of the great

Mexica rulers Tizoc and Ahuitzotl engage in ritual autosacrifice.

Aztec emperor Motecuhzoma Xocoyotzin. He offers us a physical description of the august ruler:

> [He was] about forty years old, of good height and well pro-portioned, slender and spare of flesh, not very swarthy, but of the natural colour and shade of an Indian. He did not wear his hair long, but so as just to cover his ears, his scanty black beard was well shaped and thin. His face was somewhat long, but cheerful, and he had good eyes and showed in his appearance and manner both tenderness and, when necessary, gravity. He was very neat and clean and bathed once every day in the afternoon.[13]

Complementing this is the description recalled by another conquistador who was in Motecuhzoma's presence, portraying the ruler as 'of medium height and slender build, with a large head and somewhat flat nostrils. He was very astute, discerning and prudent, learned and capable, but also harsh and irascible, and very firm in his speech.'[14] In these descriptions Motecuhzoma appears as rather unexceptional physically but impressive and worthy of respect as a king, even by his adversaries.

Looking beyond these singular descriptions, the people of Aztec Mexico were diverse in culture and language, and less so in physical attributes. They varied ethnically with overt cultural symbols: the Totonacs adorned themselves with round blue lip plugs, the Otomí wore distinctive stone labrets, the Chichimecs painted their faces with a cross-hatched design, and all groups wore characteristic hairstyles and clothing. People were also intentionally differentiated by social class: the outward trappings of elites were much more elaborate and showy than those of people of lower status. And occupation further distinguished individuals and groups, from warriors and priests to merchants, stoneworkers and farmers. This was a rich and diverse world whose complexities were daily experienced by the Aztecs and their neighbours. The newly arrived Spaniards recognized some of these variations, especially different languages and separate political affiliations. They understandably focused on kings and lords and their royal

Portrait of
Motecuhzoma
Xocoyotzin,
1584, copperplate
engraving.

trappings. In 1519 the most powerful of these was Motecuhzoma Xocoyotzin, Mexica king of Tenochtitlan and emperor of the Aztecs' known world.

The first portrait of Motecuhzoma appeared in Europe more than sixty years after the Spanish conquest of the Aztecs. It is a copperplate engraving included in an important 1584 book by the Frenchman André Thevet, a Franciscan friar, author, traveller and collector of exotic manuscripts. Thevet's Flemish engraver never actually saw Motecuhzoma, but rather drew his portrayal from textual descriptions and pictorial depictions in Thevet's collections. The famous emperor's physical features in this portrait were created by the artist following the European canon; although he does look neat and clean with 'good eyes', he does not appear as slender or as slightly bearded as the descriptions suggest. Although he has an imperial mien, with his furrowed brow he perhaps appears more apprehensive than regal. Some of his accoutrements, while embellished by the artist, follow indigenous depictions: this is especially true of the emperor's feather shield and diadem, although both of these adornments (along with the spear) have been subject to the artist's added frills such as seashells, gems and ostrich feathers. The shield would have been understood as a heraldic symbol by Europeans, but 'its feathery surface kept it exotic'.[15] Reminiscent of the 1524 Nuremberg Map, this portrait is a hybrid, the casting of an exotic indigenous individual in European terms. This sort of portraiture was commonplace at the time, and it would have been an important vehicle whereby scholarly Europeans such as Thevet moulded the impressions that their countrymen would form of Amerindians.

The Spanish conquistadores and those who followed them to the conquered New Spain grappled with the extent to which the native people were the same as or different from them. As the Spaniards marched towards Tenochtitlan they described women they encountered as beautiful 'for Indians', and identified 'so-called' priests. The Spaniards abhorred the Mesoamerican practice of human sacrifice, although practices of human brutality were well entrenched in European cultures of the time. Even so, they were unstinting in their praise of the natives' fearlessness in battle, industriousness, adaptability and skill in arts and architecture. The Spaniards would live side-by-side with the native people during the years following the conquest as they married them, tried to redefine their political and economic lives, and worked diligently to convert them to Christianity. In their turn, the Aztecs and their neighbours suffered devastating epidemics and relocations, nonetheless retaining much of their languages and cultures while adapting to the new rules and dictates of their foreign imperial overlords.

This is but a cursory overview of the landscapes, polities, people and customs that the early Spaniards saw, experienced, perceived and reported. The remainder of this book uses these along with native sources (presenting native points of view), archaeological discoveries and ethnographic analogies to reconstruct, in greater detail, public and domestic life in the greatest empire in pre-Spanish Mesoamerican history.

The Founding of Tenochtitlan, featuring an eagle perched on a cactus.

TWO

WHO WERE THE AZTECS?

The Mexicans arrived at the site of the city of Mexico, and since they liked the space and site after having wandered for many years in their journey from place to place, in some of which they had stopped for some years, having left from a distant land . . . [they] found a great stone or rocky hill, on top of which flourished a large prickly pear cactus, where a red-tailed eagle had its aerie and feeding ground . . . they decided to give the site a name, calling it Tenochtitlan . . . because of the prickly pear cactus growing on the stone, for Tenochtitlan means, in our Castilian, 'prickly pear cactus growing on a stone'.[1]

The image at the beginning of this chapter depicts this milestone in Aztec history. It was drawn by an Aztec scribe in 1540 or 1541, on the introductory folio of the 72-folio *Codex Mendoza*. This busy page is bordered by 51 blue cartouches providing a year-by-year calendrical count. This consists of four year names (House, Rabbit, Reed and Flint Knife), each accompanied by continuously cycling numbers 1–13 (yielding from the top left, for instance, the sequence of Two House, Three Rabbit, Four Reed, Five Flint Knife, Six House, and so on). It tells us that the events recorded on the page spanned from Two House (AD 1325) to Thirteen Reed (AD 1375). The scribe noted a critical religious event, the New Fire Ceremony, in the year Two Reed, or 1351. An eagle perches proudly on a cactus, calling to mind the founding story of the Mexica city of Tenochtitlan. The page not only depicts this signal event, but outlines the structure of the island city into quadrants and identifies the important men who oversaw each district. They come to us as named individuals, even though they are drawn almost identically (only Tenuch, the first ruler, stands out). The scribe painted two early conquests below the water-rimmed settlement: Colhuacan and Tenayucan. Mexica warriors with their diagnostic feathered shields subdue enemy warriors (shown smaller for effect); the burning, toppling temples symbolize conquest, and the towns' names are indicated in both pictorial glyphs and alphabetic glosses. The central image of Tenochtitlan's origin accentuates the importance of a compelling founding legend to the vitality of an *altepetl*. It situates the Mexica in time and place, and the two early conquests are preambles to an extraordinary imperial history.

Twenty years after the shock of the Spanish conquest, native scribes were still creating paintings in their conventional styles, based on their traditional knowledge. The *Codex Mendoza* in its entirety is remarkable: it records the military conquests of nine imperial rulers, the tributes paid by 38 conquered provinces, and the people's daily lives from cradle to grave. The native scribes painted the images and then described them to Spanish supervisors who added abundant glosses and annotations in Spanish script. With its multiple written components, it echoes the Rosetta Stone in its importance in deciphering the native writing system.

The *Codex Mendoza* is not only a historical document, but a material object. It was compiled on European paper and the Spanish glosses and annotations were written with iron gall ink, a Spanish introduction. But the paints used by the native scribes were local and traditional: reds and pinks from cochineal, oranges and browns from ochres, blacks and greys from carbon black, and blues and greens from composites of Maya blue and orpiment. Mixing paints for subtle colours was sophisticated, and the painters skilfully used these and other materials to create their desired pictorial impact.[2] They were at the same time artists and scribes. And the document, like the Nuremberg Map of Chapter One, was part-native, part-Spanish.

A frustratingly large number of objects from this and earlier periods have little or no verifiable history. Some objects in museums, archives and libraries are identified by tags only one or two lines long. If their histories were revealed, it might be found that their very survival hung by the barest of threads. So it was with the *Codex Mendoza*, whose eventful and precarious history is fairly well known. It is perhaps astonishing that it survived at all during the intervening 480 years. It was most likely composed in Tlatelolco, sister-city of Tenochtitlan, during the Viceroyalty of Antonio de Mendoza (Viceroy of New Spain, 1535–50). Although we do not know how long it took to compose the manuscript, the Spanish annotator stated bluntly that he was rushed at the end. This was around 1541. Once completed, it was probably carted by mule train from the highlands down the precipitous mountains to Veracruz and loaded onto a Spanish ship headed across the high seas to Spain. This ship would have sailed as part of an armed company of treasure ships, which nonetheless failed to protect it from a likely seaborne attack by French privateers. I often think, at this point, the codex could easily have been cast overboard and lost forever. But it survived.

The document never reached Spain but instead ended up in the hands of a Frenchman, André Thevet, cleric and cosmographer to the French king Henry II (r. 1547–59). Thevet signed the document in three places, twice with the date 1553. Thevet amassed a considerable collection of exploration manuscripts and valued them highly. Fortunately this codex's four subsequent owners, acquiring the document through purchase, inheritance or gifting, shared Thevet's ethos. In 1659 the codex entered the renowned collections of the Bodleian Library in Oxford, where it languished until it appeared in Lord Kingsborough's *Antiquities of Mexico* (1831–48). All along its precarious journey, the *Codex Mendoza* survived intact owing to a combination of good fortune and the conscientious stewardship of its several owners. We will draw on this document's rich content throughout this book.

The *Codex Mendoza*'s narrative history begins in the year AD 1325, very late in the long history of Mesoamerican civilizations. It is a history specifically of the Mexica, Nahuatl-speaking people who built Tenochtitlan and spearheaded the Aztec empire. To clarify, the term *Aztecs* as used here refers broadly to Nahuatl-speaking people living in the Basin of Mexico during the Late Postclassic period (AD 1350–1521). Whether we are looking generally at Aztecs in this sense or more specifically at Mexica or others, we cannot resist the question: where did these people, and their complex civilization, come from?

Predecessors

The Aztec civilization and empire (with the Mexica at its head) did not arise in a temporal vacuum: they were the last in a long train of sophisticated civilizations to rise and fall in ancient Mesoamerica. The best known of these are the Olmec of the Gulf Coast (c. 1200–300 BC), the Classic Maya of southern Mesoamerica (c. AD 250–900), Teotihuacan in the Basin of Mexico (c. AD 1–650) and the Toltecs of Tula, north of the Basin of Mexico (AD 950–1175). These early predecessors set the stage for the Aztec ascendency, developing cities with monumental public architecture, states with centralized power and elite cultures, hierarchical social arrangements, occupational specialization, vibrant trade networks, sophisticated arts and artisanship, systems of writing, complex religious beliefs buttressed by theatrical public ceremonies, and intensive agricultural techniques yielding large surpluses for growing populations. All these features associated with civilizations were entrenched in Mesoamerica before the arrival of the Mexica into central Mexico.

The Mexica consciously connected themselves to earlier venerated peoples and places in efforts to validate their role as legitimate rulers and imperial overlords in their own time. Among these early civilizations, Teotihuacan and Tula were particularly meaningful to the Mexica as they defined their own history in light of the civilizations that preceded them.[3]

The Classic metropolis of Teotihuacan, in the northeastern corner of the Basin of Mexico, lay in ruins when the Mexica first laid eyes on it in the thirteenth century. In its heyday this great city was home to as many as 100,000–200,000 people and extended over approximately 20 square kilometres (8 sq. mi.). It was unusual among most Mesoamerican cities: its sheer size was exceptional for its time, it was laid out in a grid pattern (as opposed to the more usual plaza compounds), it lacked ballcourts (a hallmark of

Mesoamerican cities) and there is no sign of the customary monuments to noteworthy rulers, priests and dignitaries. Despite these eccentricities, it was unquestionably a city that exercised strong dominion over its surrounding region and beyond.

Teotihuacan held a special place in the core mythology of the Mexica. To them, it was the sacred location where their present world was created by their gods (hence the name Teotihuacan, 'Place of Many Gods').[4] Not only did the Mexica give pride of place to Teotihuacan in their colourful mythological narratives, but they visited the ruined site and carried away physical objects; they ritually buried at least some of these (including masks, sculptures and an exquisite urn) in Tenochtitlan's sacred precinct.[5] The Mexica so revered Teotihuacan that their artists also copied and reproduced

The great Classic city of Teotihuacan.

objects and architectural designs in Teotihuacan's distinctive style, including two temples in the heart of downtown Tenochtitlan.

Tula (Place of Reeds), home to the Toltecs, lay 80 kilometres (50 mi.) north of Tenochtitlan. It followed Teotihuacan's collapse and a period of general political fragmentation, to control northern Mesoamerica (and at least influence sites to the south) from approximately 950 to 1175. The actual site of Tula, at an estimated 50,000 residents and an area of 13 square kilometres (5 sq. mi.), pales in comparison with the monumental Teotihuacan. But it would have been perfectly recognizable as a city to any contemporary visitor with its temple plaza, palace and ballcourts.

Like Teotihuacan, Tula and its people were revered and emulated by the Mexica. Toltec legends were integrated into Mexica politics and religion: these accounts blur mythology and history with their tales of temperamental gods and heroic but flawed men. The theme of glorifying a revered past prevails in these riveting narratives. The influence of the Toltecs on the Mexica was also practical. Tula was considered the origin of fine artisanship (indeed, Mexica luxury artisans were known as *tolteca*), and the Mexica replicated Toltec styles in prominent Tenochtitlan locations.[6] Tula was also exalted as the mainspring of legitimate rulership. For the Mexica, this led to an imperative for their early rulers to marry into surviving Toltec lineages to acquire a widely recognized right to rule.

The Mexica, as they entered the well-set Mesoamerican stage, were not shy about drawing on the achievements of earlier civilizations. By associating themselves symbolically and practically to Teotihuacan and Tula, they gained essential links to the glory, prestige and legitimacy of earlier sophisticated and powerful civilizations. At the same time, however, they did not abandon their singular traditional heritage as they emerged as pre-eminent players on the Mesoamerican stage.

Early Aztec History

That singular traditional heritage was initially based on the Mexica's early migratory history. The Mexica were among several distinctive groups that migrated into central Mexico from the vast regions to the north. Migrations southwards from these arid desert regions were commonplace in Mesoamerican prehistory. However, surviving historical accounts only provide details on the most recent of those migrations. In these pictorial and textual migration narratives,[7] the Mexica and several (usually eight) other named groups begin their long journey at a real or mythical place called Aztlan (Place of Herons), a settlement surrounded by water and appearing perhaps unsurprisingly similar to the Mexica's final destination of Tenochtitlan. In some accounts the groups begin their migration at a seven-lobed cave called Chicomoztoc (Seven Caves).

Collectively called *Chichimeca* (People of Dogs), these peoples lived generally nomadic lifestyles as they slowly but persistently travelled southwards into increasingly fertile regions. The groups varied markedly in lifestyle; some were more dependent on hunting and gathering of wild resources while others had acquired a good deal of the trappings of 'civilization'. The Mexica appear to have most closely resembled these latter *Chichimeca*: they wore capes (although 'tattered') rather than animal skins, and they farmed small fields of maize, built large buildings (temples), had priests, played the ritual ballgame, worshipped many deities, and were acquainted with fine luxuries such as precious greenstones and cacao. Eventful as their arrival in the Basin of Mexico was, the Mexica and many other *Chichimeca* were at least somewhat prepared for their transition from a nomadic to a settled lifestyle.

Whatever their actual starting points (which have not been definitively located on the ground), all these groups set off southwards; the Mexica were led by priests, the first of whom carried their patron god Huitzilopochtli (Hummingbird on the Left). Guided by this potent deity, the Mexica split from their travelling companions and experienced many adventures on their journey. These especially revolved around internal conflicts that probably represented real factions among the travellers but were cast as supernatural battles between competing deities. In one such event, the goddess and reputed sorceress Malinalxochitl (Grass Flower) split from her brother Huitzilopochtli and was left behind; in another, Huitzilopochtli (as the sun) takes centre stage again,

Mexica on the road in their migration. The first individual carries their patron god Huitzilopochtli.

battling and defeating his sister Coyolxauhqui (the moon) and brothers (the innumerable stars) on a hill called Coatepec.[8] It is no coincidence that in later times the Mexica applied the name of Coatepec to their Great Temple in Tenochtitlan. With its mythical aura, it would be the new centre of their world.

These historically recorded groups began to arrive in central Mexico by at least the twelfth century AD. The Mexica's early travelling companions arrived in the Basin of Mexico before them, settling among (and with) already established communities around Lake Texcoco. When the Mexica finally entered this fertile environment, it was already crowded with city-states that traced their roots to early central Mexican civilizations. Primary among these settlements were those with ties to the recently collapsed and fragmented Toltec civilization, which carried with it an aura of mythical legitimacy and political power. The people in all of these city-states lived in a constant state of political tension, with wars and threats of wars ever present: a perceived insult instantly turned allies into enemies, and a cleverly arranged marriage transformed enemies into allies. The political climate was contentious, volatile and unstable.

The arrival of the Mexica in the Basin triggered even more conflict in this uneasy political landscape. The Mexica stopped at several established places in their continuing journey, invariably annoying their hosts, moving on, visiting another community, surviving illnesses, engaging in wars and so on in their restless and seemingly endless quest for a new homeland. At one point they settled at Chapultepec Hill (source of an important spring), but were soon besieged by disaffected neighbours and fell into servitude to Colhuacan, a powerful Toltec-associated city-state. As vassals to Colhuacan, the Mexica paid taxes and served their overlords as mercenaries: at this time, others controlled their destiny.

Nonetheless, their time in Colhuacan was well spent: the Mexica gained erudite knowledge and practical experience that would serve them well in their future ambitions. They learned quickly and proved their mettle by serving the Colhua with energy and skill in Colhuacan's ongoing wars. As their reward, the Colhua gave the Mexica lands, but lands that were crawling with poisonous snakes and other lethal vermin. Still, the Mexica exhibited great fortitude by surviving this unpleasant experience, earning the respect of their overlords, who acquiesced to the Mexica elite's desire to marry one of their noblemen into the Colhua dynasty. This was a clever move, as it granted the Mexica access to the prestigious and revered Toltec heritage. However, things went sour when the Mexica sacrificed the destined Colhua bride to their patron deity (instead of conducting a more conventional marriage). On discovering this horrific offence, furious Colhua warriors drove the Mexica far into the lake. Fortunately, at that precarious moment the desperate Mexica refugees spied an eagle perched on a cactus, a sign from their god Huitzilopochtli that they had finally (and fortuitously) arrived at their destined homeland. This is the event memorialized in the *Codex Mendoza* and on the Mexican flag today.

The Mexica struggled mightily on their poor little island. They had few resources and were surrounded by antagonistic people who feared them for their fighting skills and ferocity, but respected them for their resilience and resolve. They were ragged, impoverished and despised. It was an inauspicious beginning, in the year 1325. Still, motivated by a perceived destiny and unwavering in their ambitions, they undertook a number of sophisticated strategies during the following century to boost their status in this volatile environment of highly competitive city-states and lay the groundwork for their remarkable rise to political and military supremacy. Their subsequent empire was to last nearly a century (1430–1521). Their first order of business was to make their island liveable. They began by building a humble altar of earth and wood to honour and worship their patron god who had led them to this sacred location. The island was limited in space and poor in building materials and many other essential natural resources, so the struggling newcomers went about collecting local products (such as fish, frogs, larvae and migratory birds) to trade for wood and stone. Fresh water was also not consistently available, so the Mexica built an aqueduct to divert the abundant and reliable springs of Chapultepec to the growing city.[9]

The Mexica established their central ceremonial precinct around Huitzilopochtli's altar: this modest structure, growing into the *Huey Teocalli* (Templo Mayor, Great Temple), would be partially or completely modified and enlarged thirteen times until the process was interrupted by the Spaniards. The diligent Mexica built their city outwards from their sacred core, dividing their urban landscape into quarters, each quarter further divided into numerous residential neighbourhoods (*calpolli* or *tlaxilacalli*). They managed this largely through the development of *chinampas*, lands claimed from the shallow lakebed around the island (sometimes described today as 'floating gardens', although they did not float at all). During these first one hundred years the small settlement grew into an impressive city that attracted new settlers who mixed in with the Mexica, and the island's attractive and profitable marketplace became a magnet for the brisk canoe traffic that crowded the lake. Tenochtitlan was maturing and beginning to take its place in the Basin's competitive urban environment.

A second strategy combined subservience and alliance. In 1325 their island settlement sat at the confluence of three powerful city-states: Colhuacan to the south, Texcoco to the east and Azcapotzalco to the west. Their island apparently lay in Azcapotzalco territory, and the Mexica recognized its overlordship with tributes in aquatic resources and military service. Even in the short run,

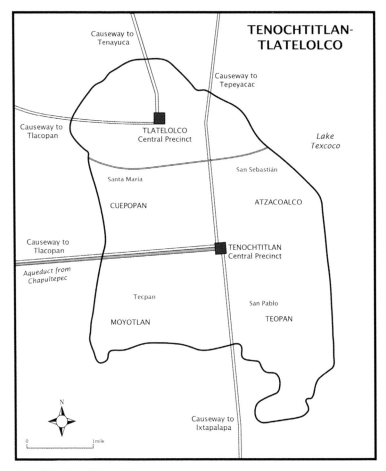

Plan of the city of Tenochtitlan.

their military service paid off. They were fierce and aggressive warriors, and their service as mercenaries to Azcapotzalco gained them rewards of lands in conquered areas. Produce from these greatly enhanced the economic base of the growing Mexica elite, contributing to their transformation from vassals to allies. They were rapidly gaining in regional political and military stature.

As a third strategy, the Mexica sought political legitimacy through shrewd elite marriages. The Mexica recognized the importance of establishing a dynastic link with the venerated Toltec lineages, and had already married into the Colhuacan dynasty, with disastrous results (as we have already seen). But relationships changed swiftly in this unstable political environment, and a Mexica leader and Colhuacan princess were again joined in marriage and had a child, Acamapichtli, who was installed as king or ruler (*tlatoani*) of Tenochtitlan in 1372. This was a decisive moment in Mexica politics: they could now claim Toltec genealogical legitimacy alongside their Chichimeca heritage. With this established, the Mexica took their place among the powerful elite of the Basin of Mexico. From this point onwards their rulers customarily married into the royal dynasties of other consequential city-states. Over time the Mexica rulers and nobility became viewed as desirable and sought-after marriage partners by these other dynasties. They had laid the groundwork for claiming an authoritative right to rule.

After approximately three generations (about one hundred years) of subservience, mercenary warfare, urban growth, elite manoeuvrings and an uncertain future, the Mexica were poised to take control of the Basin's complex politics. In 1427 Tezozomoc, the elderly ruler of powerful Azcapotzalco, died, changing the power dynamics of the Basin. As his sons vied for the dynastic inheritance, the Mexica took advantage of Azcapotzalco's divided state and threw off their overlord's yoke. The stage was set for Mexica pursuit of economic, political and ultimately imperial dominance within the Basin and well beyond. This was the destiny they so tirelessly sought.

Ethnicity and Identity

When the Mexica stepped into the Basin of Mexico they encountered numerous ethnic groups already settled in almost every niche of the landscape. There were Acolhua, Tepaneca, Colhua, Chalca, Otomí and many others.[10] Beyond the Basin resided a multitude of other distinctive ethnic groups. Among these were the Chichimeca and Teochichimeca to the north; the Matlatzinca and Michoaque to the west; the Mixteca, Zapoteca and a diversity of Mayan groups to the south; and the Tlaxcalteca, Huexotzinca, Totonaca and Huaxteca to the east. What did these names and groupings signify? What did it mean to be a Mexica? Or an Acolhua? Or a Mixteca or Totonaca or Otomí, or any of the others?[11]

Particularly relevant for the Mexica themselves was the distinction between the broad categories Chichimeca and Tolteca, essentially a distinction between 'barbaric' and 'civilized'. Although they adopted the trappings of the sophisticated Tolteca to authenticate their quests for power and expansion, the Mexica never abandoned their Chichimeca heritage and the warrior prestige it embodied; they proudly retained and displayed their Chichimeca titles and symbolism.

In historical records generally, ethnicities are most usually recorded from the standpoint of the most powerful at the time. In this case, the existing documentation (largely deriving from the early colonial period) favours the Mexica. So, for instance, we learn that the Mexica considered the Otomí to be gaudy dressers and the Totonaca to be untrained and impudent, but we know little about the attitudes of these same groups towards the Mexica.

In Aztec times ethnicities were defined by shared cultural commonalities, with little or no consideration given to biological characteristics (race). Some shared traits, such as distinctive language, clothing and other adornments, warrior regalia and hairstyles, were overt and easily recognized by all. Language was a primary means of identifying and classifying people: the Otomí spoke Otomí, the Totonaca spoke Totonac, and so on. From the point of view of the Mexica, their own language Nahuatl (meaning 'good speech') was the most refined and proper means of expression; they thought that most others who spoke Nahuatl only spoke it imperfectly, and some other groups such as the Totonaca spoke 'barbarous tongues'. This was seemingly straightforward enough, but identifying people by their language was complicated by the existence of dialects within languages and by intense interactions among speakers of these many different languages.

Clothing designs and personal adornments served as particularly visible emblems of ethnic identity: as the Mexica saw it, the Teochichimeca wore animal skins, the Matlatzinca wore coarse capes woven of maguey (agave) fibres, the Totonaca wore brightly striped capes and skirts, the Otomí overdid it with gaudy clothing, and Huaxteca men wore nice capes but scandalized the Mexica by wearing no breech clouts. Bodily embellishments such as face paint or nose, lip and hair adornments immediately identified members of specific ethnic groups. Courageous warriors who captured enemies on the battlefield were rewarded with specially designed feathered costumes and shields. Some of these, especially eagle regalia, were directly associated with the Mexica themselves. But others, most notably a costume typical of the Huaxteca, became functionally integrated into the Mexica warrior repertoire. For instance, by the time of the Spanish arrival, Huaxteca military costumes were ceremonially gifted to Mexica warriors who had captured two enemies in battle. As this was relatively common, a great many of these costumes needed to be available, and large numbers arrived in Tenochtitlan through tribute demands (even

Huaxteca warrior costume with its characteristic pointed headgear.

paid by distant non-Huaxteca people, who either manufactured or traded for them).

Hairstyles were quite complex and varied in the messages they sent: they distinguished males from females, males who had captured enemy warriors from those who had not (and were ritually ridiculed), unmarried females from married ones, and priests from everyone else. They also served as ethnic markers: valiant Otomí warriors shaved their foreheads, leaving their hair long at the back; Huaxteca and Totonaca women braided their long hair with colourful feathers and strips of cloth (which charmed the Mexica).

Ethnic emblems may seem straightforward and defining, but this was far from the case in the dynamic Aztec world. In fact, adoption of these markers could confound identities, as all of these groups (including the Mexica) were willing to adopt ethnically specific styles and designs that caught their eye. This was true of clothing, warrior costumes and even language; bilingualism was fairly common throughout central Mexico, especially among nobles. With these interweavings, it is not surprising that ethnic categories became ambiguous and blurred over time.

Other characteristics defining ethnicity were more nuanced and were based on common residence, shared history, shared destiny, common interest and common enemies. Common residence as an ethnic indicator was imperfect. Most if not all people in Mesoamerica, regardless of ethnicity, lived within the bounds of one or another city-state or similar polity. While one ethnic group may control or predominate in a city-state, most of the large communities were multiethnic and in some cases their compositions changed dramatically over time. The people in central Mexico were a people in motion, moving about the landscape through large-scale migrations such as the one involving the Mexica, or through smaller-scale, more regional movements such as those stimulated by warfare and famine, the establishment of trading enclaves, or royal invitations of renowned artisans to work in a 'foreign' city. For instance, during a devastating famine in the Basin of Mexico during 1450–54, the Mexica and their neighbours sold their families (and sometimes themselves) into slavery to people in more prosperous coastal areas; when the famine abated, many of them remained in their new homes. Similarly, during the early sixteenth century a traditionally enemy group (Huexotzinca, to the east of the Basin of Mexico) desperately sought asylum in Tenochtitlan in the face of aggression by their neighbours the Tlaxcallans; when the threat subsided and the Huexotzinca were able to return home, many opted to continue to live in Tenochtitlan. Events such as these resulted in complex, ethnically mixed communities.

Shared history and shared destiny speak to a group's past and future. Essential to the integrity of an ethnic group was an origin story and founding legend, often including an adventurous peregrination and a strong legendary leader who established a dynasty. This provided the basis for the occupation of lands (which became patrimonial) and entry into the volatile world of territorial competition and domination. With a legitimate legendary grounding, ethnic groups looked to their futures. Pursuit of a common destiny, usually promoted by a patron deity (or at least by its priests), cemented a group's activities and goals. This was particularly evident among the Mexica who proudly described themselves as destined to rule their known world by establishing their great city at Tenochtitlan and spreading aggressively outward in glorious wars of military conquest.

Ethnic commonalities were often expressed by loyalties to patron deities. So, for instance, the Otomí revered the god Otontecuhtli wherever they resided, and the Yope worshipped the god Xipe Totec even if they migrated beyond their homeland. These deities provided ceremonial reinforcement of ethnic identity in the face of a great deal of competition for an individual's loyalty and attention: household, neighbourhood, city-state, dynastic ruler, social class and occupation. Common interests sometimes entailed rallying against common enemies who posed real or perceived threats to a group. In the volatile political and military climate of central Mexico, enemies were ever-present, and although wars were most often conducted through mobilization of city-states or coalitions of city-states, some of these enterprises were boosted by ethnic cohesion.

Central Mexico was a tangled web of distinct cultures, languages and self-interested polities during this early period and continuing through the next ninety years or so of imperial rule. Individuals' loyalties lay fundamentally with their city-states, but their identities were complicated by simultaneous ethnic, linguistic, occupational and social status affiliations and alignments. Any individual's identity was multifaceted, nuanced and sometimes conflicted in the Aztec world.

The term *Aztec* does not appear as an ethnic name. Indeed, it did not appear in general usage until popularized by Alexander von Humboldt following his 1803–4 journey to Mexico. Instead, the native peoples on the eve of the Spanish conquest identified themselves by reference to their specific ethnic names or, more usually, the names of their city-states. But as the Mexica now move from their formative years in the Basin of Mexico into their imperial century, I will make more frequent use of the term *Aztec empire*, an expansionistic alliance of the three city-states of Tenochtitlan, Texcoco and Tlacopan. The term *Aztec* will also appear in reference to imperial artistic and architectural styles, and to the last of the pre-Spanish chronological periods.

THREE
Building an Empire

And the said Tizoc was extremely valiant and warlike
in battle, and before succeeding to the said lordship, he
personally performed valiant deeds in the wars, for which
he was awarded the title of Tlacatecatl. This title of high
value and rank was the point and rank from which, in
vacating said lordship, he succeeded to the said rulership,
like his brothers, father, and grandfather before him, who
took the same course and rose from that title to become
lords of Mexico.[1]

Is this true? Did this short-lived and ill-fated ruler, whose reign
lasted only five years (1481–6), actually accomplish many valiant deeds and military feats? Was he really 'valiant and warlike
in battle'? The pictorial and narrative sources offer a mixed verdict. Two documents, the *Códice Chimalpopoca* and the *Codex
Mendoza*, source of the above quotation, both list fourteen city-
states conquered during his reign, geographically scattered largely
to the west and south of the Basin of Mexico.[2] The narrative history
of the Dominican friar Diego Durán describes this king as a man
who tended towards seclusion, who failed to 'enlarge and glorify'
Tenochtitlan, and who was 'pusillanimous and cowardly'.[3] His
inglorious inaugural military campaign ended in disaster with
three hundred of Tenochtitlan's most valiant warriors lost, measured against a mere forty enemy warriors captured. In all, Tizoc
made a rather miserable showing of the ideals of Mexica military
might. It perhaps comes as no surprise that his premature death
was hastened by people around him, very probably by poisoning.

A further window into the man who was Tizoc is revealed in
the andesite stone sculpture called the Tizoc Stone.[4] This massive
monument measures over 2.6 metres (8.7 ft) in diameter and is just

under 1 metre (3 ft) high. It weighs approximately 9 and a half tons. The top of the cylinder with its representation of the sun has a shallow, round concavity in the middle (45 cm/18 in. in diameter and 15 cm/6 in. deep) and a channel running from the centre hole to the edge. The monolith probably served as a *cuauhxicalli* (eagle vessel), or receptacle for the heart and blood of warriors killed in gladiatorial sacrificial rites. It was created during Tizoc's brief reign, most likely with the intent to add majesty to the completion of an expansion of the Great Temple of Tenochtitlan (which was not finished until 1487, after Tizoc's death).[5] It was customary for each new ruler to commission monumental stones and display them in a prominent ceremonial location to glorify his reign. Apparently seven such monuments were produced from about 1450 to 1512, although only three have survived. In their day, these majestic stone sculptures were displayed as visual statements of Mexica imperial power, validating their imperial destiny. They also proclaimed the efficacy of their primary warrior gods in support of this divine mission. It was intimidation through art on a colossal scale.

An elaborate, sculpted solar disc with rays covers the top of the monument, embracing the concavity. But the sides of the cylinder command the greatest attention: fifteen pairs of military victors with their captives precede one another around the entire cylinder,

The majestic Tizoc Stone portraying military victories.

Five of the competing pairs of warriors on the Tizoc Stone. The victors wear Toltec insignia of a butterfly breastplate, feather headdress and triangular apron, and carry the *atlatl*, an elite weapon.

sculpted in sharp detail. Tizoc is the only individual identified by a personal name glyph; he is shown in the regalia of the Mexica patron god Huitzilopochtli, grabbing the hair of a man representing the city-state (or ethnic group) of the Matlatzinca, people of the Toluca area west of the Basin of Mexico. The remaining fourteen captors are dressed as another pre-eminent war god, Tezcatlipoca. All fifteen of the captors carry warrior paraphernalia associated with the Toltecs: the Mexica appropriated these objects and symbols to legitimize their right to conquest and domination, a clear message of this monument. The victims, seized and demoralized by their powerful captors, are identified by place or ethnic glyphs and wear the adornments associated with the patron deities from those locales. These earthly events of conquest (enacted by humans dressed as deities) are placed in their proper cosmic setting: above the figures runs a sky band with stars. Below the mortals, along the base, crocodilian spines and mouth bands with flint knives for teeth indicate entrances and exits to and from the underworld. It is a cosmic canvas, recreating the Mexica concept of a layered universe: underworld, terrestrial world and celestial world.[6] It serves as a model of their cosmos, identifying and solidifying the place of the Mexica in their broader, more encompassing universe.

On the surface this monument might be interpreted as a glorification of Tizoc's conquests – a tribute to his military achievements. But a closer look reveals the uncomfortable fact that only two of these conquests coincide with the fourteen listed in the two codices mentioned above (his inaugural defeat is not included on this monument). All the other conquests were claimed by earlier Mexica rulers. But perhaps we should not fault Tizoc too much: it may be that the narrative was meant to proclaim the lands controlled by him, which would include conquests already brought into the orbit of the empire. Still, it is ironic that the least illustrious of Mexica kings left behind one of the most spectacular statements of imperial military victories.

Different Rulers, Different Strategies

Tizoc was only one of six imperial rulers who expanded the Mexica domain from 1430 until 1519, when the Spaniards first set foot in Tenochtitlan and disrupted the imperial agenda.[7] These rulers descended from the earlier non-imperial Mexica kings, and their legitimacy was never questioned (although, as with Tizoc, occasionally their competence was). Likewise the Mexica's staunch dedication to imperial expansion was firmly established, and each king was expected to conform to established rules and conventions of political leadership, aggressive warfare, strategic royal marriages, earnest diplomacy, lavish feasting and participation in public ceremonies. More specifically, a 'good king' should demonstrate exceptional abilities to defend the homeland and expand the empire. He must show courage on the battlefield, pious commitment to the gods, generosity to nobles and commoners (and friends and enemies) alike, and an ability to speak well in public. He should hold an exalted military title at the time of his selection, and must be able to prove undisputed linkage to a royal dynasty. These cultural constraints and expectations did not create robotic rulers, however, since each new king brought his unique personality and individual goals to the throne. To what extent did each ruler personally influence the empire and invest it with his own special character during his rule?

Codices and sculptures of the fifteenth and sixteenth centuries offer us glimpses of some of the rulers as they undertake their essential activities. We see them statically sitting on reed thrones, vigorously capturing enemy warriors, or stoically drawing their own blood for an important ritual. But these images are highly

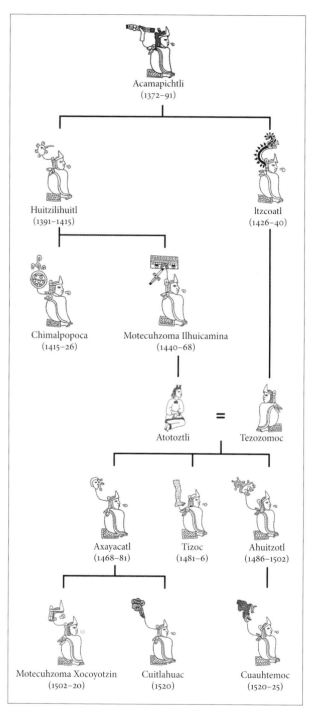

Genealogy of the Mexica kings of Tenochtitlan.

standardized and, lacking actual contemporary portraits, we must rely on narrative accounts to flesh out our views of Aztec kings, Mexica or otherwise, to arrive at a more profound sense of each ruler's personality, proclivities and goals.[8]

The first three imperial Tenochtitlan rulers, Itzcoatl, Motecuhzoma Ilhuicamina and Axayacatl, fell firmly into the mould of the ideal Mexica king. They were all adept political leaders, experienced warriors and convincing speakers, pious and generous. They all had legitimate claims to the rulership and held a high military title (*tlacatecatl*) prior to their royal selection, although Axayacatl was only nineteen years old when selected, so perhaps his military title is exaggerated. Beyond their basic similarities, subtle differences among them can be detected, primarily through their achievements.

Itzcoatl (r. 1426–40) is most renowned for overthrowing the yoke of Azcapotzalco and establishing the Aztec Triple Alliance. We can surmise that he was an opportunist (taking advantage of a weakened foe), a diplomatic master (coalescing his allies) and resolute military figure (conquering many city-states within and around the Basin of Mexico). Under this model *tlatoani*, the empire began to take form. Motecuhzoma Ilhuicamina (r. 1440–68), nephew of Itzcoatl, was already an esteemed warrior and political leader when he assumed the throne. He was a strong ruler dedicated to aggressive expansion which he undertook with gusto. He comes to us as a thoughtful man, a strategist as well as a strong battlefield commander. His military targets were selected to establish contiguous conquered subjects, gain large quantities of luxuries in tribute, and outflank his enemies. Like Itzcoatl, he performed his royal duties in a classic Mexica manner. Axayacatl (r. 1468–81), Motecuhzoma's grandson, was rather less successful than his predecessors. He mounted several military campaigns, winning only about half of them. Perhaps the Mexica's most disastrous defeat (until the Spanish conquest) came at the hands of the Tarascans to the west: when Axayacatl returned to Tenochtitlan with the meagre remains of his bedraggled army, the city wept. He was known as a stalwart warrior, but unlike his predecessors he appears to have been willing to negotiate with his enemies, establishing a number of client states along contested borderlands. His militarism was tempered with diplomacy.

Tizoc appears as a brief interlude in the Mexica's expansion-istic wave, although he did succeed in initiating a major expansion of Tenochtitlan's Great Temple. His charismatic replacement, Ahuitzotl, extended the bounds of the empire more than any other Mexica ruler, conquering city-states as far south as the present-day Guatemala border. Unlike Axayacatl, he rarely negotiated, prefer-ring hard-fought military victories. He was fearless, ambitious, heroic, impetuous and stubborn. He was also notorious for his high living, extravagant spending and willing generosity. It is prob-ably no coincidence that his conquests focused on tropical lands rich in luxuries such as fine greenstones, precious gold, shimmer-ing feathers and prized cacao. Even with these sumptuous tributes pouring into Tenochtitlan, he lived with perpetually depleted storerooms. Ahuitzotl was also notable for challenging long-standing class distinctions by promoting non-noble military men into his administration.

Ahuitzotl's successor, Motecuhzoma Xocoyotzin, continued military conquests until the arrival of the Spaniards cut his reign short. Ahuitzotl's military ambitions to stretch the empire to distant tropical lands had left numerous gaps in the imperial domain. Much of this second Motecuhzoma's reign was devoted to closing these geographic gaps, subduing rebellious city-states, and con-fronting the Mexica's perpetual and pesky enemies to the east, the Tlaxcallans. He was also highly religious, and honoured the gods as every good Mexica, especially a king, should. Being a haughty and lofty man, he concentrated on glorifying Tenochtitlan (and, by extension, himself), sponsoring the production of many majestic monuments. Consistent with his elitist personality, he immediately replaced Ahuitzotl's commoner administrators with nobles-by-birth.

All of these rulers brought their own temperaments and incli-nations to the Tenochtitlan throne. All stressed warfare and conquest, but Ahuitzotl was more bellicose than others, Axayacatl mixed in negotiations to achieve political control, and the first Motecuhzoma was a consummate strategist. Some (like Tizoc and

Motecuhzoma Xocoyotzin) were more pious than others. All but Ahuitzotl were elitist and promoted strong class distinctions. But in the end, most of the rulers' idiosyncrasies did not seem to have had long-lasting effects. Perhaps the most idiosyncratic of all was Tizoc, and he did not rule long enough to severely affect the empire's fundamental character of relentless imperial growth. Even powerful Ahuitzotl's egalitarian appointments were quickly erased by his successor.

The Aztec Triple Alliance

Each of these kings, to a greater or lesser extent, contributed to the rapid growth of the largest empire ever to develop on the Mesoamerican stage. Imperial rule was based on a tripartite alliance of the kings of Tenochtitlan, Texcoco and Tlacopan. It is often said that sharing power, especially at the top of a state (or empire), is a recipe for disaster. How did the Mexica rulers and their allies manage to maintain a coalition of powerful kings in a volatile political environment for nearly one hundred years? Fundamentally, cohesion among these allies relied on common cultural and strategic understandings, mutual respect, and collective and complementary needs.

The alliance was built on implicit and explicit agreements among the three members: segmentation and the possession of autonomous powers, the intermingling of territories and subjects, and asymmetrical hierarchies. The first of these recognized that each of the Triple Alliance kings (as *huey tlatoque*, or 'great kings') heading his own *altepetl* or city-state, controlled his own exclusive domain of other city-states without interference from the other leaders of the alliance. At the time the alliance was formed, reportedly Itzcoatl of Tenochtitlan controlled nine other city-states (largely to the south of his capital), Nezahualcoyotl of Texcoco held sway over fourteen city-states to the northeast, and Totoquihuatzin of Tlacopan ruled seven city-states towards the northwest.

These formed roughly contiguous conquest-states for each of the *huey tlatoque*, but things are rarely so simple and clean-cut. Given central Mexico's long history of back-and-forth warfare, conquests, rebellions, alliances, more warfare, and on and on, a

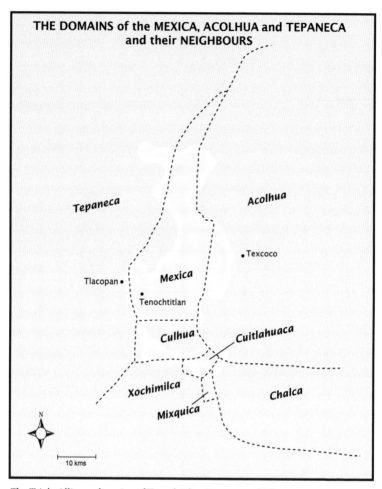

THE DOMAINS of the MEXICA, ACOLHUA and TEPANECA and their NEIGHBOURS

Tepaneca

Acolhua

• Texcoco

Tlacopan •   Mexica

• Tenochtitlan

Culhua   Cuitlahuaca

Xochimilca   Chalca

Mixquica

N

10 kms

The Triple Alliance domains of Tenochtitlan, Texcoco and Tlacopan.

complex geographic mosaic of untidy political control was almost inevitable. This complexity was exacerbated by the customary practice of rewarding prominent nobles and valiant warriors with lands (and their labourers) in vanquished regions, resulting in the fragmentation of conquered territories into the hands of many new landlords potentially from different conquering polities. In addition, each Triple Alliance ruler occasionally found it diplomatically expedient to grant lands in his own domain to another Triple Alliance ruler in the spirit of political good will and hopes of reciprocity.

At its outset the alliance was somewhat asymmetrical, with Tenochtitlan and Texcoco appearing as roughly equivalent powers, and Tlacopan the lesser partner. Over time the rulers of Tenochtitlan emphasized military power and gained clear pre-eminence in the alliance. Even in joint military expeditions, tribute obtained through these conquests entered Tenochtitlan with great pomp and circumstance before being distributed to the other alliance members: Tenochtitlan reaped all of the glory, visibly and intentionally promoting its political stature among its people and in the alliance. Reflecting these political realities, tribute distribution was uneven: reportedly Tenochtitlan and Texcoco each received two-fifths of the total, while weaker Tlacopan picked up the remaining fifth.

Asymmetry was also asserted in elite marriage patterns. High-ranking men were expected to marry more than one woman at a time (preferably several), a custom that enhanced their ability to forge political alliances through strategic marriages. But there were rules at the highest levels: the basic pattern involved a superordinate ruler offering a daughter or sister in marriage to a subordinate ruler. Their children and heir from such a marriage would therefore be the overarching ruler's grandchild or nephew. This repeatedly symbolized Tenochtitlan's superiority over Texcoco and other city-states. By extension, the Texcoco ruler, for example, married off his daughters to the rulers of his dependent city-states. While the empire lasted only about three generations, this practice was already serving to more tightly integrate city-states into hierarchies based on elite kinship.

Mutual respect was essential to a successful alliance. This was reinforced in special royal occasions such as kingly selections, coronations and funerals. Regardless of the king involved, the other two performed scripted roles: they were instrumental in validating a new *huey tlatoani*'s selection, lending stature to his coronation and honouring him at his funeral. Each such event publicly reaffirmed the strength of the alliance. Especially strong personalities also played a part. Texcoco's Nezahualcoyotl (r. 1418–72) was a larger-than-life figure and renowned as an engineer, lawgiver and patron of the arts during his lengthy reign; significantly, in 1449

Motecuhzoma Ilhuicamina called on him to design and engineer a massive dyke spanning 16 kilometres (10 mi.) along Lake Texcoco, separating saline from sweet waters and alleviating frequent flooding.

Collective and complementary needs also provided cement to the alliance. At the forefront were warfare and martial arrangements. The Aztecs lived in a military environment where the ability to amass enormous armies held great advantage; the mustering of vast armies from allied and dependent city-states boded well for victory against individual city-states. Other collective endeavours such as massive construction projects depended on cooperation among friendly city-states; the several enlargements of Tenochtitlan's Great Temple required labour and materials from several nearby polities. The Triple Alliance capitals also complemented one another. The Mexica of Tenochtitlan excelled in military strategies and engagements. The Acolhua of Texcoco were held in high esteem for their excellence in law, engineering, and arts and crafts (from poetry to pottery to painting). There is no documentation about where the Tepaneca of Tlacopan fitted into these complementary roles.

This is not to say that there were no tensions. There definitely were, especially between Tenochtitlan and Texcoco. These tensions are revealed in admittedly biased stories, such as the following. It is the early years of the empire, and the rulers of Tenochtitlan and Texcoco are jockeying for primacy in their infant alliance. In one Texcoco narrative, Nezahualcoyotl of Texcoco undertakes a campaign against Tenochtitlan's Itzcoatl, winning some rich tributary lands from the Mexica ruler. Conversely, a story from the Mexica point of view tells of a staged war in which Motecuhzoma Ilhuicamina gained lands in Nezahualcoyotl's territory, implying an honourable capitulation of Texcoco to the growing powers of Tenochtitlan. These are accounts of battles between polities that were supposed to be close allies. Whether fact or fiction, the stories suggest deep underlying frictions between these two most powerful city-states in Late Postclassic Mesoamerica.

Building and Managing the Empire

Individual city-states were the building blocks of the empire. Tenochtitlan, Texcoco and Tlacopan were *altepetl*, albeit extremely powerful ones. Allied, they pursued wide-ranging wars against other, less powerful *altepetl* that subsequently lost a measure of their political autonomy to their conquerors. This is how it happened.

Aztec military engagements were wars of aggression, not defence. The defences of Tenochtitlan were breached only once before the Spanish incursion. This occurred during the reign of the second Motecuhzoma: the Mexica's unpredictable adversaries, the Huexotzinca, crept into Tenochtitlan in the dead of night and shamefully burned a temple on the fringes of the city. The Mexica, shocked and outraged, immediately pursued revenge. Even with only this one assault on the Mexica capital, one of the *tlatoani*'s foremost stated duties was protection of his city.

Offensive military campaigns were either emphatic wars of conquest or more ritualized (although still serious) 'flowery wars'. Wars of conquest were pursued to gain control over the economic wealth (in land, labour and/or production) of other city-states. So-called 'flowery wars' were ostensibly fought to allow opportunities for warriors to practise their skills and hopefully distinguish themselves by capturing enemy combatants for ritual human sacrifice. The Triple Alliance especially targeted the eastern Tlaxcallan, Cholulan and Huexotzinca city-states for these engagements, although it appears that the wars were fought more and more in earnest, and for actual conquest, as the empire's history unfolded. Whatever the rationale, pursuing frequent wars was an accepted and expected way of dispelling any accusations of weakness by a city-state's adversaries: it publicized the willingness and readiness of a polity to pursue military encounters and dampened thoughts of conquest by other aggressive city-states. Wars also brought home captives for ritual human sacrifices, performed atop lofty temples for the satisfaction of the gods and the glorification of the empire.

The Triple Alliance economic and political agenda featured military conquest, economic control, diplomacy, intimidation,

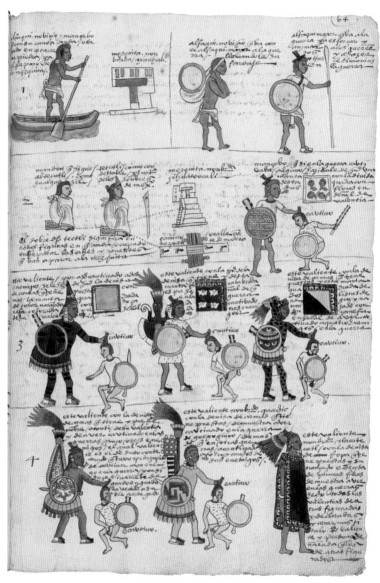

Mexica warriors capture enemies, thereby earning capes and regalia as symbols of their achievements.

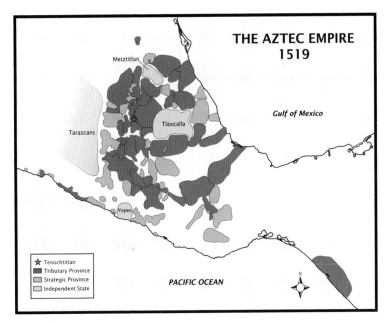

Map of the Aztec empire, 1519.

strategic marriages, and cultural and religious appropriations. Outright military conquest resulted in imperial domination of 38 regional provinces (containing a total of 271 city-states) by the time of the Spanish arrival. These were the empire's 'tributary provinces'.[9] These provinces encompassed an estimated 200,000 square kilometres (77,220 sq. mi.), millions of people, and an enormous amount of wealth in material goods and human labour. In most cases a vanquished ruler, if he survived the war, was allowed to continue in his position of power as long as he paid his regular tribute requirements, refrained from rebellion and acceded to any extraordinary demands from his imperial overlords, such as offering troops in further wars or providing labour for construction projects. Still, in some cases the imperial rulers did interfere with local politics, especially in nearby Basin of Mexico city-states where close relatives of the conquering *tlatoque* were sometimes installed in place of the traditional dynastic ruler.

Tribute assessments were negotiated and reportedly consisted of goods readily available to the vanquished people. Nearby highland subjects paid in staple foodstuffs (maize, beans, chia and amaranth) and goods such as locally available reed mats and seats, wood products, salt, bee and maguey honey, lime and deer skins. More distant provinces, conquered later, provided luxuries such as fine stones and stonework, shining gold and goldwork, brilliant feathers and featherwork, copper bells and axes, and jaguar pelts. Local specialities found here and there throughout the imperial domain included products and materials such as cochineal dyes, cacao beans, chilli peppers, eagles, copal incense, paper, gourd bowls, rubber and cotton. Provinces almost universally gave great quantities of clothing (plain and decorated, cotton and maguey fibre), and many delivered feathered warrior costumes. All these goods were carried ceremoniously into Tenochtitlan on the backs of lines and lines of human porters. They arrived on eighty-day, semi-annual and annual schedules, filling the ruler's coffers and proclaiming Mexica supremacy to mortals and gods alike. This wealth in staples, utilitarian goods and luxuries underwrote the ruler's exalted lifestyle, supported ostentatious feasts, provided glamorous gifts for allies and enemies, enhanced public ceremonies, supplied stores of food against famine, rewarded valiant warriors and financed future wars.

While control of resources through tribute assessments was a primary goal of conquest, the Triple Alliance powers also meddled with other economic matters in their conquered and neighbouring regions. Their efforts included sponsoring and commissioning long-distance merchants who trafficked mainly in fine luxuries, and tinkering with some of the major markets in their conquered regions, ensuring trading opportunities for these same professional merchants.

Diplomacy, intimidation, strategic royal marriages and appropriation of foreign symbols were all components of imperial negotiations. Whether established during a lavish feast or in a more sombre setting, non-military arrangements were invariably tilted in favour of the imperial powers. Many diplomatic efforts produced subservient city-states that did not suffer actual conquest, but were bound to the empire by notionally reciprocal agreements. This was a particularly effective imperial strategy along unresolved enemy borderlands, especially the lengthy, troublesome border

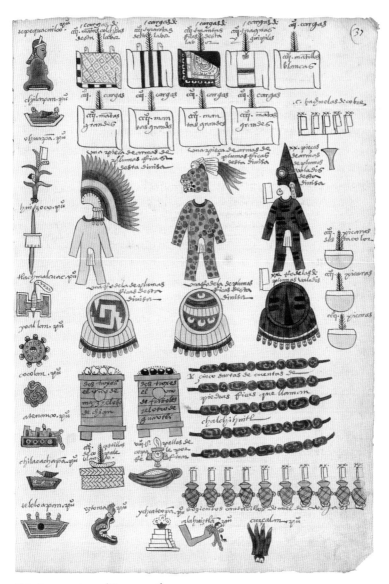

Tributary province of Tepequacuilco.

with the Tarascan Empire. These strategic provinces, resembling 'client states' established in the Roman Empire, lay along frontier borderlands, insulating the interior provinces of the empire and protecting major trade arteries for long-distance professional merchants. For their loyalty, these collaborative city-states received gifts from the Triple Alliance kings, offering these rulers gifts in return (instead of tribute). It was an alternative, less expensive strategy to outright conquest. Related strategies were brazen intimidation (for instance, where enemy rulers were invited to Tenochtitlan to view sacrifices of their own and other warriors), arranged royal marriages (already seen as working in favour of the more powerful ruler) and the appropriation of conquered peoples' religious and symbolic repertoire – from godly idols to sacred iconography to military regalia.

The empire was essentially hegemonic: loosely structured and distantly administered. Only occasionally did the victors replace conquered rulers, and only rarely did they establish provincial governors or military garrisons in outlying areas. Such additional control or oversight was typically required in habitually contentious and rebellious areas. The imperial military machine was not invincible: there were enough defeats, some of them devastating, to encourage conquered areas to rebel. But for most conquered regions, the presence of overbearing and unsympathetic tribute collectors appears to have been sufficient to reinforce imperial dominance and keep the vanquished on their tribute schedules. Warfare, violent as it was, was not intended to depopulate a conquered city-state: local survivors were necessary to assure reliable tribute payments. Still, some wars were ruinous, and on rare occasions people from the Basin of Mexico were enlisted to re-populate distant war-torn areas. In all, empire-building swooped up tributary and client city-states, protected merchants, manipulated markets, and confiscated treasured symbols. Together, these diverse strategies reveal the empire as a planned and multifaceted enterprise.

A Culture of Warfare

The Aztec empire was built on a culture of warfare. Indeed, warfare was a way of life among all Aztec-period peoples of central Mexico. All boys were raised and trained to be warriors in addition to whatever occupation they pursued in their daily lives. There were no standing armies, but every city-state had at its disposal a large body of trained warriors, who were otherwise farmers, fishermen, potters, mat-makers or other occupations in peacetime, who could be called up for military service on short notice. This did not mean that there were no professional fighting men. There were. In fact, there was a very specific military hierarchy based on numbers of enemy captures. Each capture earned the successful warrior increasingly valuable rewards in capes and warrior regalia. At the top of the hierarchy sat the elite eagle and jaguar warriors who enjoyed great prestige and fearlessly preceded armies into battle-field frays.

Wars of conquest had many recognized components and stages. First of all, there must be a justification or pretext for going to war. The volatile political environment of Late Postclassic Mesoamerica offered many opportunities for open conflict: the assassination of merchants or ambassadors on the road, a refusal to consent (or submit) to an imperial request (say, for labour or materials on a Tenochtitlan building project), balking at paying already negoti-ated tributes, or even the seemingly smallest slight or insult. If the Triple Alliance rulers directed their gaze towards a rich region, they could easily find (or fabricate) a reason to pursue its conquest.

Preparations for a military campaign, especially a distant one, were systematic and thorough. Each palace housed large quantities of armaments: offensive weapons of bows and arrows, *atlatl* (dart throwers) and darts, spears and *macquahuitl* (obsidian-studded wooden clubs), and defensive weapons of quilted cotton armour, shields and feathered warrior costumes. These were distributed to warriors prior to battle, but some combatants may have been responsible for their own weapons (and their repairs). Warriors were further outfitted with rations of toasted maize kernels, dried maize and chia seeds, sun-baked tamales, chillies and ground cacao – all nutritious, non-perishable trail food, some of which was supplied by vendors in the great Tlatelolco marketplace.

Befitting its pre-eminent military role, Tenochtitlan's king typically called the allied forces to war. Spies were sent ahead to the enemy's domain to gather intelligence on the strength of the city's defences, layout, roads and any physical obstacles, all painted on maps for Tenochtitlan's ruler. The Triple Alliance rulers assessed the 'threat' facing them and called on other Basin of Mexico cities to join them if necessary: it was paramount that the Triple Alliance forces outnumber those of the enemy.

The military contingents from each city-state marched separately to the target, under their own kings (who often participated in these wars), generals and banners. Since the men could march about 20 to 32 kilometres (12 to 20 mi.) per day, and thousands of men were engaged (including porters as well as warriors), these forces stretched a considerable distance. It took days for everyone to reach their destination. Arriving at the enemy's doorstep, each city-state army set up its own camp, was deployed separately on the field of battle, and fought as an integral unit under its own leadership and banner. Fighting, much of it hand-to-hand, was ferocious, noisy, strenuous, spirited and often desperate. It was also colourful, with warriors bedecked in spectacular feathered array leading the attack. A stated goal was to secure individual captures and thereby earn prestigious rewards, although battlefield casualties could be heavy. Battles themselves were fought in cities or on open ground. Whichever venue was chosen, victory by the assaulting forces was formally signalled by the burning of the city's temple. In essence, the attacking god defeated the defending god. Victory on the ground was reinforced by divine success.

Each war was unique, and each carried its own consequences. If successful, the victorious troops marched proudly back to their home cities, bearing loot and promises of more wealth to come. If defeated, they slunk back home and their rulers wept publicly. Even with defeats, the empire doggedly expanded through a mindset of aggression and entitled dominance, and a culture of warfare. That culture required military training for all boys, offered rewards for bravery on the battlefield, and inspired ideals and morals of courage, commitment and sacrifice in all persons. Still, despite its cultural influence, warfare was rarely a full-time job. The daily jobs of most Aztec people are the subject of the next chapter.

FOUR

MAKING A LIVING IN COUNTRY AND CITY

The good farmer . . . is active, agile, diligent, industrious: a man careful of things, dedicated . . . He is bound to the soil . . . The bad farmer (is) a shirker, a lukewarm worker, a careless worker.[1]

The craftsman (is) well instructed, (he is) an artisan . . . The good craftsman (is) able, discreet, prudent, resourceful . . . a willing worker, patient . . . He works with care, he makes works of skill . . . The stupid craftsman (is) careless – a mocker, a petty thief, a pilferer.[2]

From these quotations it is obvious that farming and crafting entailed attitudes and states of mind as well as sets of skills and knowledge. These descriptions do not stop at character, but go on to detail the hands-on activities needed to succeed as a farmer or an artisan. What did it take to be successful as a farmer, potter, weaver, mosaic maker or other producer? A close look at the craftsmanship and context of an exquisite feather shield reveals much about the artisan's knowledge, training, skills, attention to detail and mindset in fashioning this extraordinary artefact, an object complicated in manufacture and dripping with symbolism.

This round shield currently resides in the Weltmuseum in Vienna, Austria. The most convincing scenario for its life history goes as follows: the shield was made in Mexico but is first recorded as a gift to the bishop of Palencia in northern Spain around 1522, and later reappears in a 1596 inventory of the collections of Archduke Ferdinand of Tyrol (Ferdinand II) at Schloss Ambras, Innsbruck. How did it end up so far from Spain? There is a strong

Feather shield with canine and war symbolism.

suggestion that the shield may have been transferred from the Palencia bishop to Ferdinand I of the house of Habsburg in 1554.[3] Barring that, it is worth noting that the famous collector Ferdinand II was also from the house of Habsburg, as were his predecessors including Charles V, Holy Roman Emperor from 1519 to 1556. This same Charles doubled as Charles I of Spain – it is easy to see how objects from the new Spanish colonies could make their way through Habsburg relatives from Spain to Austria, and end up in the collections of Ferdinand II, an eager art collector. The 1596 inventory contained other pre-Spanish Mexican items, including a famous headdress described at the time as a 'Moorish hat' and more recently dubbed 'Moctezuma's headdress'. These objects began to see the light of day in 1884, and more emphatically in 1891 when the shield along with a feather fan, turquoise mosaic shield and feather picture of St Jerome were found at Ambras by the Mesoamerican scholar Zelia Nuttall. These objects later entered Vienna museums.

This feather shield is one of four surviving Aztec shields.[4] It measures just over 68 centimetres (27 in.) in diameter, large enough to be protective and comfortable if held by a flexed arm. The shield is manufactured of a variety of materials. The backing consists of about six hundred reed splints, bordered around the entire outside of the shield with rawhide strips sewn to the edge of the shield. This frame is stabilized by six sturdy reed sticks, four attached vertically and two horizontally to the back of the shield. A square piece of leather attached to the centre of the back protected the carrier's hand, and two horizontal leather strips held the carrier's arm in place. A further leather band could be stretched to hang the shield. A great deal of thought and care went into this generally unseen side of the shield, suggesting that structure and function were just as important as artistry in the manufacture and use of this object.

The front of the shield displays colourful, exotic feathers that adorn the rim and surface. A net of fibre threads, some dyed red, circles the entire rim. Eighteen hundred red and white roseate spoonbill feathers are tied to this netting, along with smaller feathers of the blue cotinga and green resplendent quetzal. The feathers are arranged so the red and white feathers flowed gracefully with the movement of the shield – surely a magnificent sight in a ceremony or dance. Seventy-four feather tassels hang from the bottom of the rim with a colour pattern of blue-green-red-red-green-blue. These are painstakingly fashioned of carded cotton, a cotton textile, plant fibres and five kinds of feathers, all glued and tied into colourful 9-centimetre-long (3.5 in) cones. But most striking are the feathers and gold that form the mosaic on the front of the shield. The mosaic base is formed from red feathers of the roseate spoonbill, blue feathers of the lovely cotinga, black feathers of the great-tailed grackle, and yellow and orange feathers from the Altamira oriole. The total number of feathers for this shield remains uncounted, but the feather-count of a comparable shield totals some 26,400 feathers, and may be taken as an estimation here.[5] Other materials used were glues from orchid bulbs, cochineal dyes, carded cotton, rabbit fur and gold. All of these materials, with the possible exception of the glues and the great-tailed grackle feathers, were only available from regions outside the Basin of Mexico.

The most prominent image on the shield is a blue-feathered and gold-embellished canine, most probably a coyote. The coyote carried warrior connotations, and six conquered imperial provinces were required to pay some of their tribute in coyote-style warrior costumes. While overshadowed by eagle and jaguar warriors in the military hierarchy, coyote warriors nonetheless carried a good degree of prestige: priests who had captured six enemies on the battlefield were rewarded with yellow coyote costumes with a crest of flowing quetzal feathers.[6] The coyote's association with the powerful god Tezcatlipoca also lent it special powers.[7] On this shield the animal faces another potent image: flowing water and flames (*in atl in tlachinolli*), symbolizing warfare.

What does this beautiful object tell us about its makers and their culture? It certainly exemplifies ideals of attention to detail and perfection in production. It demonstrates knowledge of diverse kinds of materials, the need for cooperation, the application of well-honed skills and an understanding of symbolic presentation. It also tells us that the artisans had access, through trade or tribute, to exotic materials from far afield. It was not bashed or pierced, so it probably did not experience the trauma of battle, but could have been flourished in ceremonies, displayed in a palace or temple, and/or offered as a gift.

Artisans like those who fashioned this shield lived not only in Tenochtitlan, but throughout the imperial domain and beyond. Some resided in palaces, their work commissioned by rulers and other nobles. Others worked in household workshops, selling their wares in marketplaces. In either case, these well-trained individuals worked full-time at their demanding craft. But the featherworkers and their colleagues still had to eat.

Producing Food

The Aztec diet

Maize was the basic staple of the Aztec diet and it came in several varieties and colours. It was complemented by many kinds of beans and supplemented by a wide variety of fruits and vegetables such as chillies, tomatoes, squashes, avocados and the fruits, flowers and pads of the prickly pear cactus. Other common edibles were amaranth seeds and greens, chia seeds and many types of greens. *Pulque* (a fermented alcoholic beverage; *octli* in Nahuatl) and cacao were popular and nutritious drinks, and cacao was also a primary ingredient in sauces (*moles*). This was not a bland diet, as salt, vanilla, bee honey, maguey honey and, of course, chillies offered not-so-subtle flavourings. In addition, domesticated dogs and turkeys (and their eggs) were eaten. For commoners this occurred on special occasions, while nobles would have consumed the animals more frequently. Rounding out the diet (especially for the lake-dominated Basin of Mexico residents) were seasonally migratory birds, ducks, wild animals such as rabbits, deer and armadillos, a wide variety of fish, salamanders and iguanas, insects and their larvae, and an edible spirulina algae (*tecuitlatl*).

Nopales (prickly pear cactus pads) for sale in a modern *tianguiz* (marketplace).

Combined, these foods and supplements provided a nutritious and well-balanced diet: maize was rich in carbohydrates; beans were high in protein; amaranth and chia were important sources of fibre, protein and minerals; and fruits and vegetables (along with maize, beans, amaranth and chia) supplied necessary vitamins and minerals (chillies have especially high amounts of vitamin C). Small amounts of meat, fish, eggs and insects added to the protein intake.

Noticeably missing from the pre-Columbian diet were many foods common on the other side of the Atlantic Ocean. These included crops such as wheat, barley and oats; the meat of domesticated herbivores such as cattle, sheep, goats and pigs; and other foods such as grapes and sugar.

Cooking was a labour-intensive and time-consuming activity. Each night maize kernels were soaked and boiled in an alkaline solution. This softened the kernels, added calcium and released the maize's amino acids. In the morning the softened kernels were ground with small amounts of water on a *metlatl* (grinding stone) into a dough or *masa*, a process that required several hours of tedious work. The *masa* could then be patted into round flat cakes and cooked on a griddle: the resulting tortillas were frequently combined with beans, chillies, meats or any other food for a nutritious meal. As an alternative, the Aztecs were fond of making creative and imaginative tamales, such as adobe brick-shaped tamales, tamales with beans forming a seashell on top, frog tamales or maize flower tamales. Maize was also boiled with water for a nutritious gruel or drink (*atolli*), and roasted and ground into a powder called *pinolli*. This was just the maize preparation. To complete the daily fare, beans were steamed or boiled, herbs and vegetables chopped, animals or fish cooked, chillies ground and sauces made and tasted. Sauces with chillies as the featured ingredient were consistently available to add spice to any meal; in addition, foods might be sweetened with bee or maguey honey, flavoured with vanilla or enhanced with salt. In a noble household a frothy cacao drink might top off a meal. As a general rule, barring famine, the Aztecs ate well.

Food preparation was women's work, and was endlessly undertaken along with spinning thread and weaving cloth, raising children, cleaning house, going to market and perhaps helping in the fields or tending a kitchen garden and a few turkeys – full days, day after day. Some women also sold cooked food in the market-places as street food.

Agriculture

The Aztecs' dietary needs were supplied primarily through agriculture. By the time the Aztec empire was in full swing, populations were growing rapidly, urbanization was increasing and agricultural lands were expanding to fit every arable nook and cranny of the landscapes. These demographic pressures were coupled with irascible and unpredictable forces of nature, including earthquakes, floods, droughts, violent storms, early frosts and vermin infestations. These occurred in the highland valleys with disturbing frequency: as examples, recorded earthquakes occurred in 1460, 1462, 1468, 1475, 1480, 1495/6, 1507, 1512 and 1513; droughts in 1332–5, 1450–54, 1502 and 1514; floods in 1449, 1500 and 1507; and pestilence in 1403, 1446, 1491 and 1506. Many of these traumatic events led to devastating famines.

To deal with these demographic and natural stresses, Aztec farmers relied on sophisticated agricultural strategies, especially terracing, irrigation and *chinampas*. Each of these was effective in a different ecological setting: terracing worked well on hillsides, irrigation enhanced yields on flatlands and *chinampas* opened up shallow lakebeds to highly productive cultivation. In all of these cases, the Aztecs managed their arable environment with an ecologically minded but nonetheless heavy hand. And in all of these cases, agricultural success was closely tied to water control.

Terracing allowed farmers to spread their agricultural enterprises up hillsides that would otherwise be uncultivable or at risk of erosion. Relatively gentle slopes were shored up with earthen embankments lined with maguey plants, while steeper hillsides were terraced with stone retaining walls. In either case, these efforts rewarded the farmer with a more stabilized soil base and increased water retention. Irrigation systems, especially large-scale canal irrigation, provided farmers with relatively reliable yields on flatter lands. By diverting natural water sources (especially from rivers and springs), farmers could expand the lands under cultivation and regulate flows of water in times of too much or too little rain. Irrigation systems required upfront investments that ranged from small-scale dams to large-scale canal constructions: some of these efforts could be undertaken by individual families or small communities, while others would have required the involvement of larger polities such as city-states.

Chinampas were a highly specialized style of agriculture, applicable in the shallow lakebeds of highland lakes or swampy tracts of the humid lowlands of southern Mesoamerica. In the lake-dominated Basin of Mexico, this technique involved defining a rectangular area with wooden stakes and 'piling up alternating layers of mud and vegetation until the plot extended about a meter above water level. The plots were stabilized by the planting of willow (*ahuexotl*) trees initially at each corner and then along the sides.'[8] These orderly plots were separated from one another by a network of canals that served as convenient canoe transportation for the *chinamperos*. By the time of the Spanish arrival, large areas of the Basin's southern lakes (fed by freshwater springs) were covered with *chinampas*. In the midst of Lake Texcoco, Tenochtitlan's small island was vastly expanded as these artificial plots spread out into the surrounding lakebed.

Chinampa fields, most of them approximately 2–4 metres wide by 20–40 metres long (6½–13 × 65–131 ft), could yield as many as three to four crops per year. This was the most highly intensive form of agriculture in Mexico at the time. Farmers enhanced these naturally fertile fields through crop rotation, multi-cropping (reducing the effects of pest infestations) and the strategic use of seedbeds (in which only hardy seedlings would be transplanted to the field). Soil fertility was maintained by dredging the canals bordering the *chinampas*, with the effect of providing nutritious muck for the growing plants and keeping the canals clear and open.

In addition to dedicated cultivated fields, people in many households throughout the empire tended kitchen gardens that produced a wide range of seasonal fruits, vegetables, herbs and flowers. A few turkeys and dogs wandered about the gardens and patios, fertilizing the gardens while being fattened for the pot.

Whatever the style of agriculture, the farmer cultivated his fields manually, his toolkit consisting of digging sticks, hoes, axes and gourds as containers. With these tools the farmer cleared the land, prepared the soil, created furrows or hills for planting, dug holes, sowed seeds, watered, weeded, watered some more, weeded again and harvested, repeating the cycle season after season and year after year. He was also armed with diligence, industriousness and knowledge accumulated from generations of farmers.

Fishing, foraging and hunting

Agricultural production was augmented by other activities, especially hunting, fishing and gathering of wild edible and medicinal plants. The Basin of Mexico teemed with lacustrine resources.[9] Fish were caught in nets; migratory birds speared or snared in bigger nets; algae, insects and insect eggs scooped from the lake's surface; and frogs, salamanders and other edible creatures speared or otherwise captured. Salt was abundantly available along the eastern lakeshore. In the Basin and beyond, apiaries harnessed the energy of bees for honey production. Wild flora, some of them cultivated but not truly domesticated, ranged from the omnipresent prickly pear cactus to a host of herbal and medicinal plants. These were often found interspersed on agricultural plots and were harvested as available and needed. Many wild animals, among them deer, armadillos, hares, rabbits and other small rodents, were captured in nets or hunted with bows and arrows.

All of these food-production and food-getting techniques yielded considerable, if not always reliable, surpluses. These surpluses allowed some persons to pursue other economic activities on full-time or part-time bases, especially the production of utilitarian and luxury material goods. Rapidly increasing populations provided manpower for these activities and a broad base of consumers for their output. Increasing commercialization of the Aztec economy also stimulated these non-food-producing endeavours, as material goods could circulate easily and profitably through the widespread network of marketplaces.

Producing Utilitarian Goods

A great many utilitarian goods were used by all Aztec households, up and down the social scale. Many of these goods were manufactured from clay, fibres and stone, although some everyday objects were made from other locally available materials. These included mats and baskets from lakeshore reeds, needles and fishhooks from copper, containers from gourds, boats from wood, weapons partially from wood, paper from fig tree bark, dyes and paints from a variety of plants and minerals, and so on. The Aztecs and their neighbours were masters at finding uses for almost everything in their environments.

People were inventive with their available raw materials, creating with them a multitude of useful objects. Ceramics were convenient for storing, cooking and serving food. Musical instruments, braziers, censers, spindle whorls, figurines, decorative stamps and a great many other objects were also made from clay. Textiles were spun and woven from cotton and maguey fibres into clothing, utility cloths, hangings, mummy wraps and a cloth that served as a form of money. Stones (from basalt to obsidian) were fashioned into objects essential for food preparation, agriculture, warfare and many other daily and periodic activities.

A great variety of tools and implements facilitated virtually every productive activity from agriculture to fishing, from house-building to mat-making, and from weaving to making pottery from moulds. Stones were especially useful in providing the raw material for tools used in myriad jobs such as cutting, chopping, grinding, pounding, scraping and hacking. Some individual tools were multipurpose and therefore in constant demand: obsidian blades cut everything from chillies to reeds to threads. A ceramic grinding bowl might be employed for grinding chillies in the morning, mashing avocados in the afternoon and pulverizing orchid glues in the evening.

The distribution of utilitarian crafts across the landscape conformed to some extent to environmental conditions. Good sources of clay encouraged nearby pottery-making, plentiful reeds in marshy areas provided a good setting for mat-making, drier areas with abundant maguey plants were convenient settings for production of *pulque* and maguey textiles, and forested areas were handy areas for woodworking. There were important exceptions, however, and some materials, especially obsidian and cotton, moved widely across ecological zones.

The production of everyday crafts was almost entirely household based. It is probable that most of this sort of production was small-scale and part-time rather than full-time in organized workshops. A common scenario was agricultural households that could bolster their income in the off-season by undertaking additional productive activities on a part-time basis. So idle farming hands might make brooms or pine torches or sandals, burnish gourd bowls, or manufacture a canoe during the dry winter months. Some of these objects were intended for use by the household's own members, others were sold in a nearby marketplace for other needed goods, and still others could end up as gifts or ceremonial offerings.

The economic investments and toolkits necessary for producing utilitarian objects tended to be small in scale; the largest investment was in education and training. As household enterprises, these crafting skills (like agricultural knowledge and

A ceramic grinding bowl.

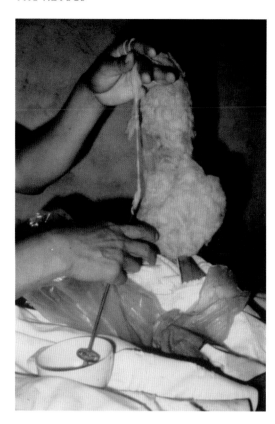

A modern Nahua woman spinning brown cotton.

know-how) were passed down from parent to child: fathers taught their sons obsidian knapping, woodworking or other specialities; mothers concentrated on teaching their daughters spinning, weaving and cooking.

Among these industries, textile production is worth a closer look. All females, roughly half the population, learned to spin and weave fibres, making textile production the most ubiquitous craft in Mesoamerica. This was time-consuming handwork. Spinning was done on a hand spindle, essentially consisting of a stick and a circular weight made of pottery or other material. Twisted and spun fibres were woven into fabrics on a backstrap loom, so called because the loom's structure (basically a bundle of sticks) was secured by a strap wrapped around the weaver's back. The patient weaver passed weft threads across taut warp threads that extended outwards from the weaver's body, creating the woven textile. A batten, the weaver's

A modern Nahua
woman weaving
on a backstrap loom.

most valued implement, tamped down the threads to form a tight weave, and any number of wooden heddles could be lifted and dropped to create simple and complex designs. It was a demanding technology that required considerable skills: girls began learning to weave at age five, finally mastering the craft at age fourteen. It was, however, a convenient household craft. The loom could be dropped at a moment's notice to care for a crying child, tend a boiling pot, greet a visitor or head off to market.

Spinning and weaving were therefore undertaken in every household in the land, whether urban Tenochtitlan or a distant rural village, and whether a commoner house or noble palace. Textile output was greater in noble households, with more women in residence. Similarly, some temples housed a cadre of priest-esses who spent much of their time weaving decorative cloths for ceremonial uses.

The weaver always had consumers, especially for articles of clothing. All clothing in Aztec Mexico was draped – that is, capes, loincloths, tunics and skirts could be worn straight off the loom. And everyone wore, and wore out, clothing. There was constant demand, and the weaver could sell her work in a marketplace, pay it in tribute, offer it as a gift to friend or god, provision her own household or wear it herself. As expected, the weaver's work was never done.

Clothing was the most common type of object paid in tribute to the Aztec overlords by their subjects, resulting in nearly 300,000 items paid annually.[10] This represented an enormous economic contribution by women in conquered regions, who also, of course, were busy spinning and weaving for their own households' needs. Tribute textiles were woven of both maguey and cotton, with maguey-fibre clothing being paid only by highland subjects. Although cotton grew only at lower elevations, even highland weavers produced cotton cloth, obtaining raw or spun cotton in marketplaces: this commodity moved widely across ecological zones.

There was a fine line between utilitarian and luxury goods. Any noble would tell you that a feather cape or headdress was a need, not a luxury. After all, it was necessary that a noble look good when walking about in public to crystallize his proper and undisputed place in the social order. Even more to the point, some production activities yielded different qualities (and hence value) of the same goods. Ceramic bowls could be rough and undecorated or fine and artistically decorated. Obsidian cutting blades were used by almost everyone for a multitude of purposes, but obsidian was also fashioned into elegant earspools or other adornments decorating noble bodies. Textiles were coarse and plain or fine and decorated. But the seemingly obvious distinction between maguey (rough) and cotton (fine) textiles was blurry, since the interior fibres of maguey plants were as delicate as silk, and even rulers were not above wearing decorated maguey-fibre capes.

Producing Luxuries

In contrast to those who manufactured utilitarian goods, luxury artisans required greater capital outlays and tended to be more concentrated in urban areas, and their work was often undertaken on a full-time basis. In addition, they emphasized precious and expensive raw materials (particularly tropical feathers, fine stones, gold and shells), and produced refined objects and adornments for gods, kings and nobles. These items included elite adornments such as feathered headgear, golden arm and leg bands, jadeite beads, warrior regalia and shields. Luxury artisans also fashioned decorative objects such as turquoise mosaics and elaborately worked textiles, and ceremonial paraphernalia such as banners, feathered litters and godly attire. Whatever shimmered, fluttered, glittered or shone was harnessed for elite and showy purposes.

None of the raw materials worked by these artisans were naturally available within the Basin of Mexico; they all had to be imported from distant lands into the imperial core. Birds such as the scarlet macaw, lovely cotinga and resplendent quetzal, with their brilliant plumage, were all native to lands to the south and along the coasts. Gold sources were scattered in the southern empire. Jaguars (with their handsome pelts) lived in the verdant habitats to the south. Jadeite came from even farther afield, in present-day Guatemala, and turquoise may have travelled from as far away as the U.S. Southwest, although recent research suggests the presence of mines within or close to the southwestern imperial provinces.[11] Beyond the rarity, difficulty of acquisition and desirable intrinsic qualities of these materials (for instance, colour, reflectivity and workability), the effort involved in transporting them over great distances on the backs of human porters added to their value. Raw materials and already fashioned objects arrived in the Triple Alliance capitals through provincial tribute payments and commercial exchanges, with merchants personally serving their rulers or operating in the numerous marketplaces throughout the land.

The ultimate destination of precious raw materials, however they moved about, was a household workshop. These could be situated anywhere, in country or city, in imperial capital or provincial centre. But they were most likely to be found in urban settings, with access to noble consumers, proximity to palaces and their resources, and availability of bustling marketplaces with their renewable stocks of precious raw materials, tools and other necessary items (such as glues, twine, abrasives, pots and baskets).

Most if not all luxury production called on all household members in the production process. Children learned from their parents, and apprentices might be brought in to augment the workforce. All of this appears to have been the case even where the artisans worked in royal or other noble palaces. For instance, Motecuhzoma's palace, in Tenochtitlan, supported at least featherworkers, goldworkers, silversmiths, coppersmiths, painters, stone cutters, greenstone mosaic workers and woodcarvers. These privileged artisans enjoyed the ruler's patronage and had access to his abundant tribute stores. They produced elegant objects specifically to adorn the ruler himself, glorify the gods and provide fine gifts to guests invited to the ruler's lavish feasts and spectacles. The concentration of these different types of artisans within the royal palace had the added advantage of facilitating cooperation. The production of a feather shield, for example, drew on the skills of woodworkers, goldworkers and painters as well as the featherworkers themselves, an efficient operation if all of these artisans lived and worked in close proximity.

Other more independent luxury enterprises were established in non-palace residential districts. These artisans needed to obtain their materials in the marketplaces or through personal contacts with long-distance professional merchants (*pochteca*). It was surely no accident that, in Tlatelolco, the *pochteca* and featherworkers lived in neighbouring districts. On a larger scale, some communities as a whole became renowned for particular crafts, notably Xochimilco for fine stoneworking, Azcapotzalco for goldwork, Tlatelolco for featherwork and Texcoco for stunning polychrome pottery.

Wherever produced, in whatever context and in whatever materials, luxury crafting followed well-tuned processes and accepted ideals. The production of a feather shield or a turquoise mosaic disc required more than one artisan. A well-honed division of labour is documented for featherworkers, and similar arrangements were very likely followed by those who fashioned stone mosaics. For instance, girls were trained to discern fine shades of colour, boys were put to work making glues and other members of the household arranged the thousands of little feathers or stones into designs, all of this surely supervised by a master artisan. The feather shield speaks for itself, as does this turquoise stone mosaic disc. The disc measures 32 centimetres (13 in.) in diameter and contains more than 14,000 little turquoise and other stones, carefully arranged to yield subtle shadings and intricate designs.[12] Some of these stones are barely larger than a pinhead. Given the complexity of the design, the artisans also demonstrate a knowledge of religious symbolism. Undoubtedly the entire design was laid out, revised, laid out again, tweaked here and there, laid out again and so on before finally being glued to its wood backing.

This level and proficiency of workmanship required intensive training and expert skills, passed down from parents to children. It also demanded the mindset and morality described in the

A turquoise mosaic disc discovered in a cave in central Mexico.

quotations at the beginning of this chapter: the workers, men, women and children, exemplified qualities of care, patience, resourcefulness and attention to detail. They strove for perfection. Luxury artisans also exhibited a frugal side: some of the stones in the turquoise mosaic disc were clearly recycled from other objects. A good artisan must in addition be trustworthy and honest, especially in interactions with others. These are, of course, ideals, and some artisans fell short, being inept, lazy, dishonest, careless and destructive.[13] Such individuals presumably were not employed in palaces (or at least not for long); nor were they likely to have been successful in more independent settings, competing with more adept craftpersons.

Artisans were not the only non-agricultural workers in the Aztec world. There were innumerable specialists, including priests, merchants, administrators (such as ambassadors and tribute collectors), teachers, astrologers, water collectors, barbers and porters. There were lofty rulers and their grand entourages. There were people who did not actually make things, but rather worked with or enhanced things: builders, masons, sculptors and painters. This was a society of intense economic specialization and resulting interrelationships: farmers sought out potters and mat-makers, merchants needed porters, rulers required fancy clothing, and everybody needed constant sources of food and the periodic services of priests. All people in the Aztec world depended on predictable means of obtaining and exchanging goods and services, which leads us to the world of bustling markets and energetic merchants.

FIVE
MARKETS AND
MERCHANTS

It will not be useless to hear what happy money they use;
for they have money which I call *happy* . . . This money
is produced by a tree . . . The natives call the fruit and the
tree by the same name, *cocoa* . . . These trees and coins
only grow in certain regions . . . Merchants, therefore, visit
them and carry on their trade by means of exchange. They
bring maize, or cotton for making clothing and also made
garments, in exchange of which the people give them cocoa.[1]

Cacao beans. Large white cotton cloaks (*quachtli*). Thin copper axes. These three very different objects have one thing in common: they were all used as money in the Aztec world. Some, more than others, also served practical purposes.

Specific money-objects such as these facilitated exchanges in the many marketplaces of the realm. Among them, cacao appears to have been the most common and served dual purposes of practical utility and currency. Cacao beans were grown on trees in the humid lowlands of Mesoamerica, along both coasts, and on into Central America. Cacao trees are (and were) finicky: they require year-round warmth and humidity, are vulnerable to local diseases and vermin, need overarching trees that house tropical forest midges for pollination, and thrive best as dispersed plantings along stream beds. The trees produce pods that contain a sweet white pulp and thirty to forty almond-shaped beans. Humans, most interested in the bitter beans, compete for the maturing pods with small animals such as monkeys and squirrels who seek the juicy pulp. The trees traditionally provided two harvests annually. Extracted from the pod, the beans were fermented, dried, roasted and winnowed (the outer shell removed). The beans were now ready to be ground into a usable powder or circulated as money. Cacao was prepared as a chocolate drink, or as a sauce primarily consumed by nobles or by the general population at special events requiring feasting. The Aztecs added water to the ground cacao and poured it back and forth to create a bubbly foam. The bitter taste of cacao was offset by adding maize, vanilla, honey, achiote, allspice, various aromatic flowers or chillies – the last used in a sauce (*mole*) that is still popular today.[2]

Cacao beans were also used as a form of money. Aztec money literally grew on trees. There were several types of cacao, and at least two different types were paid as tribute to the Aztec empire. They apparently varied in quality as a drink, and it is possible that some types were used for consumption while others circulated as money. That said, cacao beans clearly were used as a widely accepted medium of exchange in marketplaces throughout the Aztec world and beyond. They were abundantly available and appear to have operated as small change, mostly for utilitarian goods: for example, early Spanish accounts record valuations of

Cacao pod with white pulp encasing the beans.

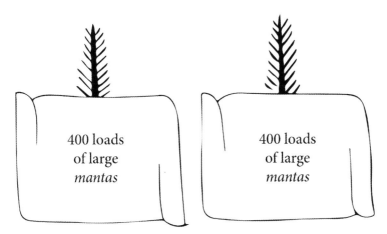

Quachtli, large cloths or *mantas* that served as high-end money. The images on top of each cloth indicate the number 400.

one hundred cacao beans for a turkey hen, thirty for a small rabbit, four for a large salamander, three for a newly picked avocado, and one for twenty small tomatoes or one large tomato. A market-goer could purchase one tamale for one cacao bean.[3] These equivalencies probably varied according to the type and condition of the beans, and as commodity monies, probably also responded to seasonal availability and other circumstances. Despite their relatively low value, cacao beans attracted the attention of counterfeiters who sliced the outer covering of the bean, removed the inside, inserted other substances such as sand or ground-up avocado pits, and deftly sealed the opening.

Large white cotton cloaks were woven by women and were widely available throughout the Aztec world. They carried a specific name (*quachtli*) and were in a category by themselves. For highland weavers, the cotton needed to be imported from lowland fields. These specific cloaks, fully woven, were paid in tribute to the Aztec lords in quantities amounting to as many as 53,600 per year. We do not know if they were also worn or displayed, but their use as a form of money is well documented.

These cloaks served as a high-end medium of exchange and standard of value. They could be used to buy slaves, to ransom certain slaves or to provide restitution for theft. An individual's wealth was expressed in terms of *quachtli*: a person (probably a

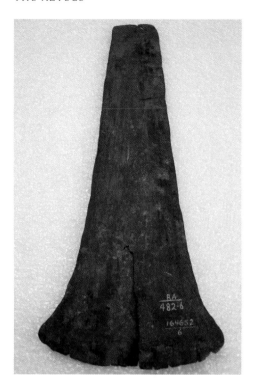

Thin copper axes, a form of money.

commoner) could live for one year on twenty of these cloths.[4] We do not know the exact size of the cloaks, and indeed their size and quality may not have been strictly standardized: one report values different grades of *quachtli* at 65, 80 or 100 cacao beans, while another account states that 65–300 cacao beans could purchase one cloak, the value varying with the quality of both the beans and the cloak. Monies, yes, but flexible, commodity monies.

Copper axes range from paper-thin items to heavier varieties. The thin objects are often found stacked in caches, geographically distributed in the southern and southwestern part of the Aztec empire and beyond (Oaxaca, Guerrero and Chiapas). These thin axes were unsuitable for practical use, but heftier varieties may have served utilitarian purposes. Two provinces in southwestern Mexico paid copper axes in tribute to the Aztecs, although we do not know if they were the thin or thick variety. The copper itself may have been produced and processed in these areas, but copper was also available further west in areas controlled by the Tarascan empire, sworn enemies of the Aztecs. Trade transcended these tense political borders.

Copper axes are described as relatively low-value currency in early colonial sources.[5] Their use as money may have been concentrated in the southern part of the empire. Similar regionalization may explain the mention of several other commodity monies such as copper bells, red shells and stone beads in southern Mesoamerica.[6] To confuse things further, the Spanish conquistador Bernal Díaz del Castillo interpreted quills filled with gold dust as a measure of value for cloaks, slaves or gourds full of cacao in the Tlatelolco marketplace.[7]

People used these commodities throughout the Aztec world and beyond to facilitate economic exchanges and promote their social and political agendas. Most of these transactions took place in the many lively marketplaces throughout the realm.

The Marketplace (*Tianquiztli*)

Marketplaces were the primary settings for the exchange of goods, services and news. They have a long history in Mesoamerica, pre-dating the arrival of the Aztecs in central Mexico and still thriving today in towns and cities throughout the country. A few of the largest marketplaces, such as that at Tlatelolco, enjoyed permanent covered stalls as well as a sprawling outdoor marketing space. However, most were completely open-air affairs, vendors laying out mats in the community's plaza in the morning and carrying away their leftovers at the end of the day.

In Aztec times people were able to find a bustling marketplace in any city-state capital (and often other towns) to sell their surplus goods and purchase necessities and luxuries for themselves. A market outing was also an eagerly anticipated opportunity to pick up the latest news and rumour, large and small: was a war in the air? Did those expected merchants arrive from the south with bright colourful feathers and polished green stones? Did they catch the thief from last week's market? That couple who ran off together – did they finally get married? Market day served as the local and regional newspaper, from the news page to the social section.

Marketplaces varied considerably in schedule and size. The biggest markets, serving large urban areas, met daily but attracted greater activity every five days (one Aztec week). The great Tlatelolco marketplace, a short walk from downtown Tenochtitlan, reportedly hosted 20,000–25,000 people on a daily basis and 40,000–50,000 people every fifth day during its 'big' market.[8] This was exceptional. Other marketplaces, whether within the Basin of Mexico or beyond, served their immediate region and attracted merchants from more distant areas; they tended to draw fewer people. Some of these were the venues for known specializations: the Acolman market was famous for dogs, Coyoacan was a centre for wood products, Otompan and Tepepulco for turkeys, and Azcapotzalco and Itzucan for slaves. Texcoco was the place to go for ceramics, gourds and fine cloth. Some markets operated in a coordinated region, each community hosting a market on a different day of the week: the five participating communities shared market responsibilities but also reaped the economic and social benefits from the gathering together of large numbers of people from different communities. Other markets, many of them on the fringes of the Aztec empire, resembled medieval European fairs, meeting every twenty days (one Aztec month) and offering a wide range of utilitarian and especially luxury goods. Long-distance merchants, who largely trafficked in valuable items, targeted these borderland markets for their many eager consumers and predictable profits.

Even specialized marketplaces offered a wide range of other goods and services. Spanish conquistadores, touring the extraordinary Tlatelolco marketplace before the city's decimation, provided long lists of its offerings. One Spaniard, Bernal Díaz del Castillo, finally gave up on his list, stating that 'I shall never finish if I tell it all in detail.'[9] Many materials and goods for sale were unfamiliar to the Spaniards. A look at the market list compiled by native people fifty years after the conquest reveals some of these products;[10] they included all of the foods, utilitarian goods and luxury wares discussed earlier, and many more. Subsistence staples such as maize and beans and every known supplementary food and flavouring were for sale. Baskets, bowls, griddles, ropes, clothing, sandals, obsidian blades, firewood, pitch pine for torches and innumerable other objects were needed in every household and required frequent replacement. Farmers could find digging sticks and axes; sculptors mulled over available stones and chisels; weavers and painters selected brilliant dyes and paints; priests and their assistants found incense, pottery braziers and slaves. A man planning a feast easily found jugs and jars, turkeys and dogs, tobacco and tobacco tubes, sauce bowls, cacao, salt, precious clothing for gifts, and perhaps a slave or two. A merchant seeking a profit studied shimmering feathers, gleaming jadeite stones, tiny turquoise tiles, fine gold and exotic shells. A hungry shopper headed for the fast food section. There was something for everyone.

Every vendor abided by well-established marketplace rules. Each type of good was sold in its designated area: food in one, wood products in another, clothing in its own corner, and exotic luxury goods in yet another. Some of these arrangements were practical: at Tlatelolco, heavy, bulky goods such as stone and lumber were piled up at the periphery of the market, probably along a canal. Consumers seeking a particular commodity knew exactly where to head upon entering the plaza, and could readily and critically peruse all the offerings available on that day. A marketplace stone (*momoztli*) marked the centre of the marketplace, serving as a religious shrine and the focus for public proclamations. Off to one side sat the marketplace judges, keenly surveying the smooth running of the day's transactions and ready to exact justice on any improper or criminal behaviour. The judges' constables roamed the rows of vendors, alert to any infringement of rules of sale, whether cheating by a vendor or filching by a passer-by. Their vigilance might be rewarded with the discovery of a cacao bean counterfeiter. They might uncover tainted foods: a 'bad' maize vendor hid fetid and mouse-gnawed grains beneath good ones, a 'bad' bean seller mixed infested beans with good ones, and a 'bad' chia vendor tossed chaff into his pile of seeds.[11] Falsified measures might be exposed (goods were sold by measure and number, but not weight). For these and other violations, justice was immediate and unsympathetic. Measures were broken, wares confiscated and thieves taken into custody on the spot.

How did sales and purchases actually take place? In the first instance, prices needed to be established, and these were usually resolved through bargaining or haggling. Prices fluctuated regionally, annually, seasonally, daily, even hourly, and bargaining allowed flexibility to both buyer and seller. When maize was recently harvested and abundant, prices favoured the buyer; when hostile enemies blocked trade routes and interfered with supplies of luxury goods, prices favoured the merchants as artisans competed for the scarce items. Vendors were sensitive to the scheduling of known periodic ceremonies, anticipating needs for extra quantities of goods for flamboyant ceremonies and obligatory offerings. One could expect a spike in the market availability of gourds and chillies for the monthly ceremonies of Huey tecuilhuitl, an excess of brooms during Ochpaniztli, and an abundance of little red feathers during Toxcatl. Bargaining also allowed a fruit seller to get a high price early in the day as he hawked perfect, unblemished fruits; that same fruit seller might offer his remaining well-ripened produce more cheaply at the end of the day, to avoid carrying it back home.

Once a price was established, the customer had to then pay for the hard-fought purchase. Most exchanges relied on barter, the exchange of goods/services for goods/services. The parties may agree on one small pot for three tomatoes, a container of salt for five chillies, a bunch of flowers for a load of firewood, and so on. This may have been the predominant method of exchanging goods, but what if the commodity needs of buyer and seller did not coincide? Did the transaction fail? Enter universally (or at least widely) accepted money forms to facilitate commerce. As discussed at the beginning of this chapter, cacao beans, large white cotton capes and thin copper axes all qualified as objects accepted as currency and perhaps as standards of value. Producers and merchants conveniently exchanged these objects as monies and as commodities in marketplaces throughout the empire and beyond.

The marketplace was colourful, noisy and competitive. Sellers vied for the attention of customers by loudly hawking their wares and making their displays as attractive as possible. Most of these vendors attended markets near their homes. People such as barbers, porters and even prostitutes moved about the marketplace

Modern copal resin being sold by measure in the Tepoztlan marketplace.

seeking business. Other vendors established themselves on a mat in an appropriate part of the plaza: many of these arrived with small surpluses from their fields, the lakes, their household crafts or their kitchen gardens. They sold maize, fish, turkey eggs and other foods; pots, baskets and gourd bowls; herbs and medicines; nets and digging sticks; and woven cloth and clothing. Obsidian-sellers worked on-site, fashioning blades to order. No household was completely self-sufficient, and vendors were also consumers on market day.

Professional Merchants

Travel and transport in pre-Spanish Mesoamerica was entirely on foot or in canoes. Foot transport was facilitated by a tumpline that stretched across the carrier's forehead or shoulders, supporting a basket or carrying frame. Loads of about 20–25 kilograms (50 lb) could be carried with this apparatus. Canoe traffic provided efficient transport on lakes and rivers, and along coastlines.[12] Canoes crowded the Basin of Mexico lakes at the time of the Spanish arrival, transporting large numbers of people and goods between lake-shores and islands (including the bustling Tlatelolco marketplace).

Whether on foot or by canoe, Aztec transport depended on human energy and successful trips were necessarily contingent on season, weather conditions, terrain difficulties, political hindrances and perhaps any unlucky encounters with determined thieves.

Most marketplace vendors sold small quantities, carrying their own goods on their own backs or in their own canoes. They usually travelled short distances to familiar marketplaces, enjoying the day with friends, neighbours, relatives and others. Collectively they offered almost all the products of the land. These producer-sellers were the mainstay of every market and essential to the sustained welfare of every household.

Other sellers attracted particular attention from market-goers. These were the professional merchants who moved medium- to high-value goods across ecological boundaries and from distant lands. Some arrived at highland markets from lowland regions laden with cacao, cotton and fine salt; they were especially popular with noble consumers. Other merchants carried precious, exotic and expensive goods from areas deep inside the empire and beyond. These latter were the *pochteca*, long-distant professional merchants who served as private entrepreneurs and state agents.

Pochteca were a fixture in every major Mesoamerican city. They lived in exclusive neighbourhoods of at least twelve Basin of Mexico cities, including Tenochtitlan. These specialized districts or *calpolli* provided strong support groups for merchants whose lives were hard and laden with risk. Heading off on a perilous journey, the travellers were advised:

> Thou mayest perish in the midst of the forest (or) the crags; thy poor maguey fiber cape (or) breech clout dragged forth; thy poor bones scattered in various places . . . As thou goest, go dedicated, indebted, to misery – suffering . . . endure the unseasoned, the saltless, the briny (food); the dried tortillas, the coarse *pinole*, the wretched, soggy maize.[13]

They faced hunger, thirst, exhaustion, dismal weather, and theft and assassination on the road. To offset these dangers and increase their chances for success, these merchants often travelled in large caravans, requiring the service of a great many porters. Some of these were slaves who could be sold at either end of the journey. They all might dress as warriors if entering rebellious or enemy territories. Indeed, there were occasions when the merchants engaged in battles far afield. It was not a cushy or idle life.

Under these conditions, the *calpolli* offered economic security and room for social advancement to each individual merchant. The groups were exclusive: the merchants educated their own children in the trade, administered their own social hierarchy and in general protected their members and their property. Members took care of their own: persons unable to travel gave their goods to those who could, and reaped the benefits of a successful expedition. Essential rituals sending an expedition off or receiving the tired travellers home were sponsored and attended by fellow merchants. An ambitious merchant seeking personal renown and political position would receive economic and moral support from his fellow merchants in sponsoring an expensive feast and offering one or more slaves for sacrifice at a public, state-wide ceremony.

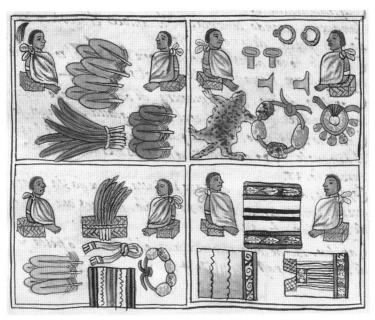

Wealthy merchants display fine textiles, precious feathers and valuable stone adornments.

These merchants relied on marketplaces as outlets for their expensive wares. They brought exquisite clothing, glamorous feathers, precious stones, slaves and other high-end goods from distant regions to the Tlatelolco marketplace. Likewise, they carried other goods (from golden adornments for nobles to rabbit hair and obsidian tools for commoners) to distant lands, always with an eye towards profitable exchanges. They traded in marketplaces throughout the empire and beyond, circulating high-value goods across geographic zones and cultural regions.

Professional merchants also contributed to the religious life of the community. A prosperous merchant, accumulating wealth through successful trading ventures, was expected to dedicate some of that wealth to the enactment of public ceremonies, thereby contributing to the community's spiritual well-being. This usually involved expensive feasting and the offering of a slave for sacrifice. The slave alone could cost as many as thirty or forty *quachtli*, depending on his or her dancing skills. The merchant's feast was lavish, with high-ranking merchants and nobles attending as honoured guests. It required, in one example, at least eight to twelve hundred precious cloaks and four hundred decorated loincloths as gifts; eighty to one hundred turkeys; twenty to forty dogs; bins of maize, beans and chia; a great many tomatoes, chillies and squash seeds; forty to sixty jars of salt; twenty sacks of cacao beans for drinking; and three to four boats of water (1 boat of water = 1 small cape = 100 cacao beans). And this does not include the necessary and innumerable amounts of charcoal, firewood, baskets, cups, dishes, serving and sauce dishes, copal incense, flowers, tobacco and hallucinogenic mushrooms that provided popular culminations to some feasts.[14] These were extraordinary expenses – everyone critically appraised the merchant's outlay, and he dared not be stingy. The *pochteca* were not only economic actors, but were willing to exchange their considerable wealth for social advancement and political clout.

In that vein, some *pochteca* directly served their rulers by trading royal goods with foreign rulers: these were diplomatic as well as economic transactions. They also penetrated restless and enemy areas disguised as spies and armed as warriors. And they officiated as judges in the grand Tlatelolco marketplace. In short, these privileged merchants served as state agents both at home and abroad. Being closely associated with Aztec rulers and political expansion, it comes as little surprise that these highland merchants were not particularly popular as they travelled and traded in distant lands. They were always vulnerable to attacks on the road, and murderous assaults on them served as frequent provocations (or excuses) for imperial aggression. However, the benefits must have outweighed the dangers since they avidly persevered in supplying Aztec rulers and noble consumers with essential status-linked luxuries, and connecting highland rulers to rulers of lands beyond the imperial thrall.

An International Economy

In 1502, the year that Motecuhzoma Xocoyotzin rose to the Mexica throne in Tenochtitlan, Christopher Columbus encountered a large native trading canoe at the Bay Islands off the coast of present-day Honduras.[15] The canoe was manned by Mayan merchants, and it carried diverse commodities: obsidian knives and swords from highland Mexico, cacao beans from the humid lowlands, bronze axes and bells from the faraway Tarascan realm, and fancy textiles probably from temperate and hot lands. Not only did these commodities range widely in value – the merchants were dealing in relatively cheap goods alongside expensive wares – but they hailed from great distances. Clearly the people of Aztec-period Mesoamerica moved goods over great distances and across often contentious political borders and distinct cultural orbits.

Some of this trade was 'down-the-line', moving from nearby marketplace to the next nearby marketplace, some goods eventually travelling in this manner over long distances. Local producers and long-distance merchants all contributed to this sort of trade in foods, utilitarian goods and luxuries. Professional merchants also targeted specific trading areas far from their homelands, stopping at large markets along their route but focusing their commercial efforts on a distant land renowned for its precious products.

These trading areas qualify as international trading centres: commercially attractive and relatively safe trading locales. Here,

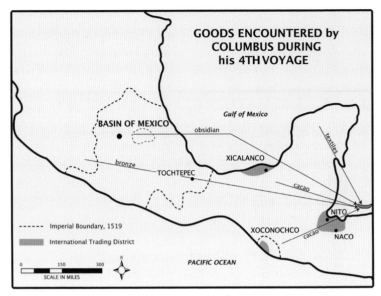

Map of goods transported by canoe that Columbus encountered during his fourth voyage to the Americas.

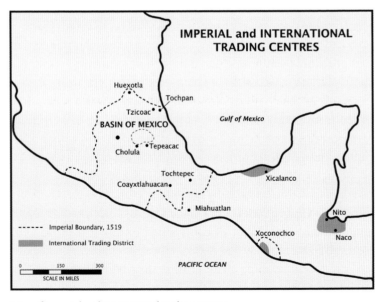

Map of imperial and international trading centres.

on the fringes of the empire and just beyond, merchants from far and wide traded with one another in animated marketplaces overseen by wealthy rulers. They were strategically located between environmental zones or political domains, were accessible by well-trod trade routes or canoe ports, and were places where international, regional and local-level trade intersected. Some of these centres, such as Tochtepec, Huexotla and Nito, housed more-or-less permanent enclaves of foreign merchants.

One international trading centre, Xicalanco on the southern Gulf coast, especially attracted Mexica *pochteca* who received armed escorts on the last legs of their journey. Here, the Mexica merchants carried their ruler's goods for trade (and negotiations) with the local ruler, exchanging fine cloaks for precious green-stones, turquoise mosaic shields, tortoiseshell cups, shells, wild animal skins (probably jaguar) and a wide variety of exotic, colour-ful feathers. On their return to Tenochtitlan, all of these luxuries were delivered directly to the ruler – the merchants were his emis-saries. But the merchants also had their own interests in mind, carrying their private goods for trade in Xicalanco's marketplace or along the route to and from the coastal centre. Profit was never far from the merchant's mind.

Other international trading centres dotted the borderlands of the Aztec realm: Huexotla in the northeast was renowned for the availability of fine salt, and nearby Tochpan held a celebrated fair every twenty days with a bewildering selection of fine goods. Xoconochco on the southern Pacific coast was the place to go for cacao and exquisite fineries such as shimmering feathers; this region was conquered by the Triple Alliance in the 1480s but continued to be an attractive trading destination as well as a tribute-paying province. Cholula in the eastern highlands offered valuable merchandise such as 'jewels, precious stones, and fine featherwork'.[16] Cholula was also a noted pilgrimage centre, attract-ing visitors from far and wide. Farther afield, Nito and Naco (on the present-day Gulf of Honduras) offered cacao and other low-land fineries.

While trading at these international centres was carried on at all levels, periodic arrivals of *pochteca* provided a special economic stimulus with their wide range of expensive wares and attitudes toward profit-making. They also facilitated high-level political ties as diplomatic envoys, carrying political messages sealed with exchanges of material wealth. Throughout the empire and beyond, they were pivotal economic players in an increasingly commercialized world. And, more subtly, they also influenced the Aztec volatile political landscape and dynamic social setting.

Professional merchants were rising stars on the Aztec stage. They were commoners by birth but wealthier than some nobles. They suffered harsh conditions to secure (for a price) the showy luxuries so desired by the materially hungry nobility. That same nobility felt threatened by this 'new wealth', and the merchants in response often deemed it necessary to play down and even hide their affluence. They occupied an ambiguous and uneasy position between the glamorous lives of the elite and the more humble circumstances of commoners. In the next chapter we will see how all of these people acquired and maintained their social positions, up and down the social hierarchy.

SIX

NOBLES AND COMMONERS

Adjoining those temples or enclosed within them were palaces, great halls, and apartments for different kinds and qualities of persons. On entering the door, each one knew his place, according to his rank. The great men had their own palace, the knights theirs, the hidalgos their own, and the squires theirs also . . . Their rules were so rigorous that under pain of death no common man dared pass the threshold of the royal houses and chambers. For the servants who brought water and firewood, therefore, there were secret doors, separated and very distant from the main one.[1]

Motecuhzoma Xocoyotzin's palace was such a place, as seen in the *Codex Mendoza*. The five 'doughnuts' decorating the top of the palace identify the building as a palace, or *tecpancalli*. The king himself sits in state on his throne (a reed seat), wearing a turquoise cloak and turquoise diadem as symbols of his exalted nobility. Two rooms, one on either side of the king, are reserved for neighbouring allied kings: rulers were known to visit one another on special occasions and must be housed appropriately. At the front of the palace, steps lead up to a courtyard, the far end of which is dignified by the king's dais. Many other rooms, here left to the viewer's imagination, graced the sides of the courtyard and housed libraries, armories, tribute goods, clothing, musical instruments, ceremonial regalia, shrines and meeting areas for warriors and judges. These last rooms are shown on either side of the entry stairway. The scribe includes some activity here, as very vocal male and female litigants appeal to the king's panel of judges (was this perhaps a marital dispute?).

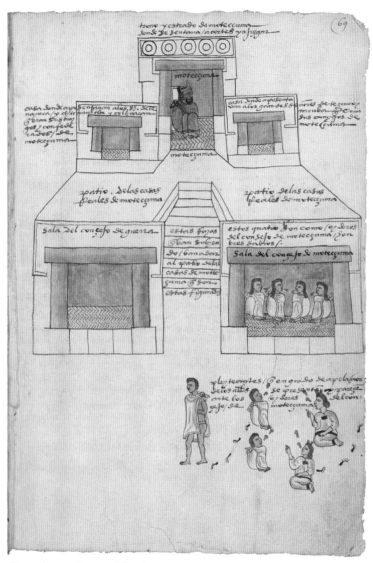

Motecuhzoma Xocoyotzin's palace.

The scribe of this page has retained many native artistic styles, including depictions of seated individuals and speech scrolls, footprints, reed mats, symbols of royalty, and hair and clothing styles. Still, he has been influenced by introduced European artistic conventions, in this case, depth and perspective (not used in pre-Columbian Aztec art). He has made a valiant effort, but nonetheless the shape of the palace appears a bit awkward – he is still learning this skill.

This image of a royal palace is consistent with other documentary descriptions and actual palaces on the ground, revealed by archaeological investigations. However, not shown in the *Codex Mendoza* depiction are the ruler's domestic quarters, whose warrens of elegant rooms were arranged around additional courtyards. A palace, after all, was both home and administrative nerve centre for kings and other high-ranking nobles; any city-state with a dynastic king would have one or more of such buildings.

Palaces were extraordinarily large, walled, raised on platforms and constructed of the finest stones and other materials (including aromatic woods such as cedar). Open spaces and rooms would have been elegantly appointed with colourful decorative hangings draped over walls and doorways, textile awnings, mural paintings (red was a popular colour), mosaics, large ceramic braziers for warmth and pine torches for light. Intricate featherwork, such as the feather shield seen earlier, might further embellish the elegant setting. There was, however, little in the way of furniture: reed mats, wooden and stone benches, and storage chests seem to have sufficed. One or more of the domestic courtyards would have featured a *temazcalli* or sweatbath for use by the residents.

Every palace also encompassed expansive orchards and fragrant gardens with ponds, fountains and other pleasurable features. A ruler might have more than one palace, some of which were 'pleasure palaces' designed for hunting, horticultural experiments or just relaxing from a stressful job. A king must always appear regal, and an exalted noble must always display his supremacy: palaces were critical ingredients in buttressing these elite public auras.

The day-to-day running of such an expansive and complex establishment required a large cadre of bureaucrats in the administrative area and a large number of wives with a multitude of servants in the domestic realm. The palace was home to the ruler or noble and his immediate household (wives and children), but it is not clear how many of the numerous palace workers actually lived in the palace. It is likely that the ubiquitous servants and slaves were housed within it. Whether living in or arriving from the outside, on any given day people from all walks of life were present in the palace. Tribute accountants managed and dispersed goods, overseers of labour assignments received their daily orders, palace-sponsored artisans worked diligently and leading merchants saw to their entrepreneurial interests. There were gardeners, cooks and weavers. Someone had to maintain the fires, sweep the floors, serve the meals, clean the clothes and manage the loads of products (such as firewood and vegetables) carried from the nearby marketplace to the palace for daily use. Repairs of 'this' and 'that' were inevitable and ongoing. Warriors talked strategy, judges judged and the lord's private bodyguards handled palace security. In Motecuhzoma's palace, at least, hundreds of caretakers were responsible for the ruler's exotic animals and birds.

These were the 'ordinary' days. Levels of activity peaked when foreign dignitaries visited and were lavishly feted, when state-sponsored merchants returned laden from a successful trading venture, when the ruler prepared for war or returned from an extended military expedition, or when the palace was decorated for a major ceremony. Anticipation heightened when a midwife arrived for the birth of a child.

With hundreds of people milling about daily, and even more on extraordinary days, palaces were beehives of activity. Importantly, they were venues where the loftiest citizens to the most humble intermingled and worked side by side.

The Social Hierarchy

Aztec society was highly stratified. Everyone knew his or her place, even what door to use when entering a palace. Rulers sat at the top, slaves at the bottom, and different ranks of nobles and types of commoners in between. All of these statuses were clearly defined in terms of rights, responsibilities and codes of behaviour. But they were also linked together and people from all walks of life depended on one another for everyday and exceptional needs.

Kings

It was good to be king, ruler of an *altepetl*. Palatial life was comfortable: rooms were luxurious, gardens were gorgeous and fragrant, food was plentiful, clothing was elegant, and wives and children were numerous. Servants were everywhere to see to your every need. Public adoration was satisfying and expected, even if in some cases ill-deserved. The king went to war, took centre stage at many public ceremonies and sat in state in his palace, greeting nervous visitors and meting out justice. He basically ran the business of government for his city-state; the three Triple Alliance kings additionally governed as imperial rulers. In the event of an imperial conquest, a vanquished city-state king came to owe allegiance and pay tributes to an overarching king, resulting in a system of ranked kings. But whatever their imperial standing, city-state rulers dominated a steep social hierarchy and enjoyed society's most elevated lifestyles.

Kingly perquisites came with high moral expectations and weighty practical responsibilities. First and foremost, a ruler must be an eloquent speaker (after all, the title *tlatoani* means 'speaker'). He was supreme protector of his domain and must be ever vigilant. He must lead in war and demonstrate bravery on the battlefield. On political and ceremonial occasions he must flaunt his wealth, build spectacularly and look ostentatiously magnificent: intimidation was a significant ingredient in displays of power. He was expected to make wise alliances, often sealing them with marriages to close relatives of other kings. Since kings and other nobles practised polygyny, a great many alliances could be cemented with a great many marriages. And, finally, kings must always be just and generous: the most loved and respected rulers meted out justice fairly, opened their storehouses in times of desperate need and honoured ceremonies that included gifts to the poor. We have already seen that some kings were more successful than others at meeting these expectations.

The practice of polygyny resulted in a great many children, all of them anticipating lifestyles and jobs appropriate to their highborn status. As examples, Nezahuacoyotl, king of Texcoco from 1418 to 1472, reportedly fathered 117 children; the sixty sons were all granted lands along with the labour of commoners to work those lands. Nezahualpilli (r. Texcoco 1472–1515) supported all of his 144 children with wealth and prestigious positions. These were expensive legacies. Polygyny and its resultant progeny also created certain household complexities. Wives were ranked depending on their own ancestries, and their children were also ranked. Yet of these many children, only one could become the next king, fertile ground for simmering political intrigues.[2]

Other nobles

What was to become of all these other royal children? And, for that matter, what happened to the children of other nobles, present in every city-state? They were all nobles, and were groomed to occupy positions as the king's advisors and as governmental ambassadors, tribute collectors, judges, military leaders, bureaucrats, accountants and scribes. Teachers, priests and other occupations requiring an elite education were also suitable as noble career paths.

Nobility was attained through fortuitous birth, an estimated 5 per cent of the population enjoying that status. The primary criterion for noble status, birthright, had been operating in central Mexico for generations before Aztec imperial expansion, causing a rapidly growing elite class. Nobles were not a monolithic status or group. Instead, they were ranked. The highest-ranking nobles lived in glamorous palaces and managed great estates, dressed elegantly and enjoyed many of the benefits of rulers but on a smaller scale. Some of these acquired exalted titles, partly based on their favoured birthright (including their mother's status) and partly based on their own personal attributes and accomplishments. Others came to occupy prestigious jobs in the political, military and priestly hierarchies, occupations requiring an education largely restricted to the aristocracy.

Nobles (the king included) were expected to serve as models of exemplary moral high ground. They were also handed positions of importance where success or failure could have serious consequences not only for the noble himself but for the city-state as a whole. A general may make astute or erroneous decisions on the battlefield, a judge might decide an important legal case with wisdom or ignorance, a priest might enact a ceremonial performance perfectly or not, or a tribute collector may be tempted to skim off some of his ruler's goods. Those who failed to meet the high standards of noble morality and behaviour were punished severely in the courts.

Kings and other nobles visibly affirmed their elevated social positions. To this end, the Mexica king Motecuhzoma Ilhuicamina (r. 1440–68) enacted a number of sumptuary laws, or explicit rules of rights and behaviour attached to specific social statuses. These appear to have been in full force under the second Motecuhzoma as well (although relaxed under his predecessor Ahuitzotl). Among the laws, cloaks of specific designs were reserved for nobles of specific ranks, only nobles were allowed to wear long cloaks, and cotton clothing was to be worn only by the aristocracy (others were to wear maguey-fibre clothing). In addition, only the highest rank- ing nobles were allowed to wear earplugs, lip plugs and noseplugs fashioned of gold and fine stones. Only rulers and high-ranking nobles were permitted to dance with gold and feathered rattles, arm bands and anklets. And to accentuate their elevated status, nobles were received in their own designated rooms in the ruler's palace.[3]

These were all highly visible criteria, openly distinguishing nobles from commoners (and different grades of nobles from each other). Infractions of these rules by unprivileged persons would

Quetzal headdress dubbed 'Moctezuma's headdress'.

be easily recognized and were harshly punished. Even so, there were exceptions, and these are discussed below.

Commoners or macehualtin

A commoner was any non-noble, and it was commoners' hard work that made possible the extraordinary lifestyles of nobles. Comprising an estimated 95 per cent of the population, commoners engaged in essential occupations such as farming, fishing, craft production, construction, entertainment, trade, transport and all manner of services. The term *macehualli* (pl. *macehualtin*) means both 'commoner' and 'subject':[4] in addition to providing for their own livelihoods, they also paid goods and/or labour services to the state, to their noble overlords and to their communities.

Nobles and commoners were readily distinguishable from one another by appearance and general living standards. Nobles dressed elegantly, commoners humbly. Nobles lived in large, beautifully adorned buildings; commoners resided in more modest dwellings. Household goods were on the whole more elegant and abundant in noble households than in commoner ones. And while nobles could celebrate life cycle ceremonies with lavish amounts of cacao, flowers and tobacco, some commoners could only celebrate with stale tortillas and 'old, withered flowers'.[5]

These are broad generalizations, and commoners' living circumstances actually ranged from destitute to fairly affluent. Their houses could consist of a single-room dwelling or a group of rooms arranged around an open-air courtyard. These latter could house more than one nuclear family, allowing relatives to live in close proximity and pool their labour and skills. This was particularly convenient for crafting households that required a diversity of skilled workers. Whatever the household's occupation, daily domestic life in multi-room arrangements was focused on the patio, with the surrounding rooms used for cooking, eating, sleeping, storage and protection from the elements.

Archaeological investigations in several Aztec-period communities throughout central Mexico have revealed considerable size variations in commoner houses: single-room houses ranged from 20 to 77 square metres, while multi-room dwellings ranged from

A commoner's humble house.

40 to 416 square metres. These size differences reflect the number of occupants and possibly household affluence. Sizes of agricultural plots also varied greatly, from 4 to 1,377 square metres in Tenochtitlan's *chinampa* areas, and from 92 to 8,701 square metres in a district of Texcoco.[6] More reflective of affluence is variation in construction materials, from wattle and daub to adobe and stone, and from dirt floors to those covered with a lime plaster. Differential affluence can also be seen in the types and quality of household goods. One would expect plain, ordinary pottery and little or no jewellery in commoner houses, yet despite sumptuary restrictions, some fine goods such as polychrome pottery and jadeite jewellery have been found archaeologically in commoner houses. These few examples illustrate the considerable wealth differences among people classified monolithically as commoners.

Some affluence differences can be attributed to the life cycle of the household: a family with small children will generally struggle more than a family with grown children who can contribute economically. Affluence can also be tied to occupation. Professional merchants and luxury artisans could become very wealthy, even surpassing some lesser nobles. Some fortunate workers may have been compensated rather grandly: in one instance, sculptors employed by the Tenochtitlan royal palace were paid with loads of clothing, squashes, beans, chillies and cacao ahead of time, and two slaves, two loads of cacao, one load of cloth and some pottery and salt upon satisfactory completion of their task.[7] The receipt of slaves, cloth and cacao would have been a boon to the economy of these sculptors' households.

Commoners also differed in access to political power. In general, they had little or none. Most commoners lived in residential *calpolli*, which offered them stability in the form of strong kinship bonds, access to communal lands, focus on a patron deity, attendance (for boys) at a local military school, and often a common ethnicity. Some of these *calpolli*, notably the professional merchant and luxury artisan districts, enjoyed a high degree of cohesion and special favours from their rulers. Whether artisans or farmers, *macehualtin* owed their loyalty to their city-state ruler, and perhaps to an overarching, conquering ruler. That loyalty was expressed in three primary ways. The first was military duties. Since there was no standing army, any man might be called to war at any time (hence the local military schools). Second was tribute, or payments in goods to the city-state or imperial lord. And third was corvee labour, which directed commoners to projects such as construction of roads and walls, repairs of temples or clearing of canals. Other commoners, called *mayeque*, owed their loyalty and tribute payments directly to the noble on whose lands they toiled. Their

Commoners receiving their labour duties from an overseer.

standard of living and tribute and labour duties closely resembled those of *macehualtin*; they were instead paid to a local noble.

While occupying the bottom of the social hierarchy, commoners were not entirely powerless. There are accounts of commoners playing city-state rulers against one another for their own benefit, and of warriors pressuring their own king when denied looting opportunities during a distant conquest. These uprisings enjoyed a few recorded successes, and kings and nobles were aware that their considerable powers faced some constraints. At the same time the social system was not hopelessly rigid, and opportunities were available for people to both rise and fall within the hierarchy.

Up and Down the Social Scale

Once a noble, always a noble; once a commoner, always a commoner. These seemingly straightforward statements mask the underlying dynamics within the Aztec social system. The culture offered prescribed avenues for moving up the social ladder, and also specified circumstances in which an individual could lose social status.

Gaining status

An unknown number of people achieved noble or quasi-noble status during their lifetimes through their own exemplary efforts. The most usual avenue was through success on the battlefield, whereby a man (noble or commoner) could gain increasing renown (and material gifts) with each enemy capture. Among the Mexica, these gifts were bestowed on the valiant warrior by his ruler during public ceremonies and consisted of specifically designed cloaks and warrior costumes. These cloaks and feathered regalia sent pointed messages: everyone knew that a man wearing a shell-motif cloak had captured three enemies in battle, and enemies facing off on the battlefield recognized a jaguar-clad warrior as an intimidating adversary indeed. With four captures, jaguar and eagle warriors enjoyed the added privilege of constituting a war council and meeting in designated jaguar and eagle houses, prestigiously located to either side of the Great Temple in Tenochtitlan. Additional captures afforded opportunities for further advancement in the military hierarchy. Achievements on the battlefield allowed commoners to break through some of the society's sumptuary laws: they could wear jewellery (although of inexpensive materials such as bone or wood) and could adorn themselves while dancing, and a warrior with wounds on his legs could wear a long cloak.

Distinguished standing through military advancement pertained only to the warrior himself – he could not pass it on to his offspring. This matter of quasi-noble status may have been somewhat unsettled: Ahuitzotl favoured elevating commoners to high administrative positions; his successor Motecuhzoma Xocoyotzin retracted that policy and allowed only nobles (including noble children) to serve his administration and his royal self.

A further way of gaining status involved acquiring extraordinary wealth, and transforming that wealth into prestige and social position. This was particularly relevant for the professional merchants, or *pochteca*. Wealthy *pochteca* were expected to host lavish feasts and offer slaves for public sacrifice, both extremely costly investments. In exchange, they acquired prestige and position within their merchant *calpolli*, along with royal recognition.

A third avenue for gaining high position was through the priesthood. The Aztec religion contained many deities; each deity was housed in its own temple and celebrated with its own ceremonies, and each temple and ceremony required its own cadre of trained priests (and, to a lesser extent, priestesses). Deities and their temples were ranked, and so were priests; opportunities abounded for advancement within the priestly hierarchy. But first and foremost, priestly duties demanded a specialized and prestigious education. Since such an education was largely restricted to noble children, priestly positions and advancement tended to favour nobles by birthright. At the top of the priestly hierarchy, the highest-ranked priests commanded the dual sanctuaries of Tenochtitlan's Great Temple and administered the most flamboyant ceremonies in the city. Ceremonial events at the Great Temple sometimes turned political, as with the mass sacrifices of warriors during the dedication of an expansion of that temple in 1487. These priests were front and centre on that stage.

The military. The merchants. The priesthood. These appear as mini-hierarchies within the overall Aztec social hierarchical scheme. They all allowed for upward movements of individuals with lofty aspirations. But people could also fall, sometimes precipitously.

Losing status

An individual was born in a designated slot in the social system, but we have already seen that there was some fluidity in that system, allowing people to rise to levels above their position at birth. By the same token, people could also lose status. Some of these were nobles. With noble polygyny, large numbers of children were produced, but few titles and prestigious jobs were available to pass out among them. Low-ranking nobles – youngest sons of youngest sons of youngest sons of a titled, estate-owning noble – were still nobles (*pipiltin*, sing. *pilli*), but they had slipped away from the titles, jobs, lands and other generators of wealth and no longer completely enjoyed the perquisites of noble standing. Most were attached to their aristocratic relatives' households. But if they had political or other ambitions, their best hope was to enter the military or priestly hierarchies.

A more serious social demotion was slavery. Slavery involved a loss of social and economic freedom, to varying degrees. In most cases slaves were expected to work hard, but they were legally free to marry and largely establish and maintain their own households. Others lived directly in the households of their 'owners'. Women could contribute to a household's economy by endlessly spinning and weaving, and men might engage in field work, tool-making and other domestic chores. Sahagún's statement that slaves 'became someone's digging stick and tump line' suggests that slaves were, expectedly, given the hardest jobs.[8]

We also find slaves being sold by merchants in marketplaces. In some cases these were intractable slaves who could be sold on the open market. Slaves' good behaviour was encouraged by the well-known fact that they could be sold to merchants or others for purposes of ritual human sacrifice.

There were two types of slaves. First were warriors captured in warfare. A primary goal of battlefield tactics was to capture enemies

A schematic of a market, showing slaves with their wooden restraints. A female slave spins thread.

for ceremonial sacrifice; these hapless individuals were held in captivity in the victorious city until the arrival of a propitious ceremony sealed their fate. They did not enter the social lives of their captors in any other way, although captures in war may have yielded some slaves who survived to work for their conquerors. An example is the wife (probably wives) and child (probably children) of a vanquished ruler who were taken to work in the conquering ruler's palace.

People, nobles or commoners, men or women, adults or children, could arrive at slavery by other routes. Slavery was an ignoble social status allowing few rights, but it did provide some luckless individuals with a sort of safety net. One pathway involved extreme poverty. Individuals with no other social or economic option could voluntarily sell themselves to more affluent people, receiving food, clothing and living space in return. This could occur on a large scale under conditions of severe drought, famine or other natural calamity. The most extraordinary example is that of the devastating four-year famine in the mid-1450s, when poor highland people, as a last desperate measure, sold their children to prosperous merchants and nobles, and even to the Totonaca of the Gulf coast who were not affected by the famine. The Totonaca traded maize for their human purchases. This occurred in the year One Rabbit, and it so seriously traumatized the Mexica and their neighbours that they continued to dread the Rabbit years in future generations.

Another route into slavery was through excessive gambling. Gambling was frequently associated with games such as the ball-game and *patolli* (similar to pachisi), and even the king enjoyed partaking. The ruler could undoubtedly cover any losses, but for lesser people gambling could be ruinous. Losing everything of value, obsessive gamblers may eventually gamble themselves (essentially their labour) in a final desperate wager. Additionally, slavery was a known punishment for theft, especially of low-value goods such as maize seeds or a turkey. In these cases, the thief was required to work off the value of the theft in the service of his or her victim.

All was not lost if you were a slave. In the first place, slavery was not typically hereditary (although there does appear to have been an ancient form of hereditary slavery). Second, people who sold themselves or members of their family for purposes of survival may have been able to buy themselves and their family members back in brighter times. The economic dimension of slavery is also explicit in people's loss of freedom through gambling and theft. In both cases, slaves harboured the hope that they could accumulate enough resources to eventually buy their freedom. How much might that cost? For a theft, the value of the goods stolen would be required; for gambling, it is most likely that one's freedom could be obtained for the value of the gambling debt. As

A conquered ruler is strangled and his wife and son are taken as slaves. Note the wooden collars.

previously mentioned, one source suggests that a person (probably a commoner) could live for a year on twenty *quachtli* (large white cotton cloaks).[9] This may serve as a general standard of living, and hence the value of a person's annual labour. There were also possibilities of escape: despite the restraints of rigid wooden collars, if a slave could flee through the marketplace and reach the house of a local official, he or she would be granted their freedom. Onlookers, however, must take care – anyone interfering with the slave's escape could be enslaved in his or her place, suggesting some degree of fairness in this frantic spectacle. Treatment of slaves must have varied considerably. We do know that there were cultural inhibitions on mistreating slaves, and all slaves could look forward to the day One Death when they could expect to receive special, respectful treatment. This was also the day on which individuals who had been unjustly enslaved were freed.[10]

In sum, Aztec social stratification was complex, dynamic and moderately flexible. Social positions were fundamentally established through birthright, with power and wealth concentrated at the top of the hierarchy. But few (if any) social systems are so straightforward, and here we find shadings, discontinuities and ambiguities. Poor nobles overlapped in wealth with prosperous merchants. An established noble could descend into slavery through a gambling obsession. Or a warrior, priest or merchant could harness their own abilities and ambitions (and perhaps catch some luck) to attain social positions beyond their birth. Wealth and status did not necessarily go hand-in-hand: there were poor nobles, wealthy merchants and luxury artisans. Still, all positions entailed moral, family and community responsibilities, and a person gained nothing if he or she did not adhere to the cultural norms and goals of the society. These moralities and priorities, instilled through education and reinforced through legal institutions, are the subject of the next chapter.

SEVEN

TO BE A PROPER
AZTEC

> They went saying that on earth we travel, we live along a mountain peak. Over here there is an abyss, over there is an abyss. Wherever thou art to deviate, wherever thou art to go astray, there wilt thou fall, there wilt thou plunge into the deep.[1]

This graphic description of life gone amiss encapsulates the Aztec view of their existence, which was precious, precarious and unpredictable. Only by faithfully adhering to the culture's exacting moral pathway could a person, noble or commoner, maintain a steady journey along life's 'mountain peak'.

The *Florentine Codex* is the source for this chapter's initial quotation and image. As discussed earlier, this monumental textual and pictorial document tells us a great deal about Aztec moral life, laws, crime and punishment. Although composed about half a century after the Spanish conquest, the written Nahuatl accounts and scribes' images on these topics largely represent pre-Spanish indigenous practices. The quotation above reflects characteristic Nahuatl narrative style, and the illustration below depicts people, things and a title glyph in native style.

The consequences of failing to follow life's proper pathway were severe. If a case were particularly difficult to resolve, it was brought before the ruler himself and his highest-ranking judges. The defendant in this case has obviously been judged guilty (of what we do not know) and sentenced to death by the king's executioners. One of these is specifically identified by his title glyph in the upper right corner: Quauhnochtli (*quauhtli* = eagle, *nochtli*

A malefactor receives the ultimate punishment.

= prickly pear cactus). The man is strangled, but could have been sentenced to death by stoning, slashing or beating.

The man seated on the left is a ruler or one of the exalted judges involved in the case. His high status is revealed by the diadem floating above his head and the reed seat on which he sits, symbols identifying both kings and judges. He is most likely one of the judges, his cloak being the best clue: other judges in this document wear the same flowered cloak.

The defendant in question appears to be a commoner (from his plain cloak), but the text of the document indicates that he was an official. Even judges, among the highest-ranking people in the society, were not immune to Aztec justice. The same man sitting in judgment, if he was lazy, favoured his friends and relatives, became drunk, or even was just incompetent, could be condemned to death by the ruler and executed by these same executioners. There was a fine line between morality and law in Aztec society; law, essentially, was the codification of the society's moral precepts. Both laws and moral principles defined proper behaviour, and an encompassing system of justice enforced those codes – to everyone in the society.

The Moral Pathway: Right and Wrong

The Aztecs had strict moral codes. The watchwords for their design for living were respect, humility, moderation, honesty, energy and hard work. These moral codes provided pathways to the fulfilment of personal ambitions and societal expectations. Conforming individuals who followed these principles for an exemplary life also contributed to the integrity of residential groups and the maintenance of social statuses. On a grander scale, attention to these ethical standards was intended to avoid upsetting the all-important natural and cosmic balance.

Each of these moral principles was manifest in behavioural expectations. For example, male nobles were taught that respect was central to the Aztec way of life: a person must obey orders willingly, recognizing and accepting his rung on the social ladder. He must not act haughtily (except, apparently, for the king himself, who was expected to flaunt his superiority). Respect of social position, supported by humility, was of paramount value. Additionally, moderation required that a proper noble present himself in public as a model to all: he must walk deliberately – not too fast but also not too slow. When speaking, he must moderate his voice and speak slowly and pleasantly. He must be prudent with his food and drink, neither gulping nor breaking his tortillas into little bits. And he must dress decently, neither pompously nor in rags. Honesty buttressed the other values and was reflected in the need to relate truthfully and fairly to others. Embezzlement, cheating and fraud were serious offences. Judges carried weighty responsibilities and were required to mete out justice without bias, on pain of death. More informally, it was not a good idea to eavesdrop or gossip, as it made a man look foolish, and gossip was an offence meriting imprisonment (since it fostered social discord). A man must be energetic, manifest in the demand that a person must not oversleep, and must respond quickly when called. He must not be considered as 'perverse, lazy, languid, negligent', at risk of being severely disciplined.[2] And hard work was not confined to commoners: nobles were also expected to work hard, although not so much in manual labour. Whatever their occupation or activity, they must not waste time; an idle person would be obvious for all to see. And finally, at all times they must pay attention to their noble lineages and respect their ancestors.

Similar moralities were expected of noblewomen. Translated into behaviours, noble girls and women needed to respect others, with humility, and be devout to the gods. It was especially important for them to protect their noble lineages and legacies, and particularly horrendous if they brought any dishonour or embarrassment on their families or ancestries. They must be moderate, as evident in the need for females to be as conservative as men in their clothing, to dress neither gaudily nor in tatters. Likewise they were to be gentle in their speech, tranquil in their travel and serene in their manner. It was also important that they exhibit honesty in several dimensions. In addition to basic truthfulness, women were expected to be true to their work: it must be done with care and devotion. Sloppiness was unacceptable.[3] Also unacceptable was an unseemly relation with a man outside of wedlock – the importance of chastity was strongly instilled in young girls. And finally, energy and hard work were hallmarks of the woman's world, whether she be cooking, spinning, weaving, sweeping, caring for children, marketing or making offerings to the gods.

A particular virtue (and goal) of nobles, male or female, was to not behave like commoners. Furthermore, Mexica nobles were admonished to not be 'untrained, stupid . . . greedy, shiftless . . .

and gaudy dressers' like their neighbours the Otomí, or 'crude, pompous, and cowardly' as they viewed another ethnic group, the Tlalhuica.[4] Disgraceful behaviour for a Mexica. Yet many of their stated moralities were shared with those of lower status or different ethnicity. Like nobles, commoners were expected to exhibit respect, humility, moderation, honesty, energy and hard work. They were required to respect nobles and the deities, and, importantly, their peers; respect was a pervasive feature of Aztec culture. Behaving humbly was not a huge problem for commoners, most of whom lived in humble circumstances anyway and could not afford lavish lifestyles. Exceptions, as we have already seen, were the professional merchants who were sufficiently wealthy to enjoy an elevated life-style but who displayed humility before members of the nobility. This demeanour appears to have been a kind of survival strategy on the part of prosperous, ambitious merchants to avoid the jealousy of nobles by birth.

As with nobles, moderation and honesty were hallmarks of commoner values and behaviour. And, as the backbone of the Aztec economy, commoners were expected to work hard and per-form with diligence and energy. The industrious farmer and meticulous artisan described in Chapter Four are good examples of these ideals. Qualities of energy and hard work especially define a commoner woman: she was 'strong, rugged, energetic, wiry, very tough – exceedingly tough, animated, vigorous; a willing worker, long suffering . . . resolute, persevering . . . She gives of herself. She goes in humility. She exerts herself.'[5]

All persons, male and female, noble and commoner, were expected to conform in all arenas of life, whether they be house-hold, state or supernatural. Household harmony could be disrupted by dishonesty, adultery and especially drunkenness, which was often considered to be at the root of many other mal-feasances. The state order was particularly threatened by people who ignored sumptuary rules – rules that reinforced social and political hierarchies. Commoners who attempted a lifestyle above their station (by wearing fancy cloaks or appearing in a 'noble wing' of a palace, for example) violated the visual messages of hierarchy and power, leading to social and political ambiguities.

Diligent farmers and lazy farmers.

At the highest level, gods were certainly affronted by a lack of proper attention to prescribed rituals and might inflict the offenders with particularly unpleasant diseases or deformities. At all levels, an individual's most advisable path to a successful life was to diligently follow the 'exemplary life' of acceptable moral codes.

The culture's emphasis on moderate behaviour does not mean that a warrior was not expected to be loud, fierce and bellicose on the battlefield, or that a king was not expected to be gaudy in dress and pompous in demeanour. Or that a high priest could not conduct human sacrifices atop lofty temples amid noisy and flamboyant ceremonies. Ideals were guidelines for behaviour, and rather than being absolute, they were to some extent situational.

Fate

Where did responsibility lie for one's behaviour? One's own good or poor decisions? Adequate or incomplete socialization? Abundance or lack of opportunities? Luck? Or the workings of fate? In the Aztec world view, at least some of one's life story was laid at the feet of fate.

Fate was not random or capricious. Rather, it entailed specific guidelines against which individuals could make important decisions. Those guidelines were embedded in a ritual calendar of 260 days (*tonalpohualli* or 'count of days'). This calendar consisted of twenty distinct day names meshed with the numbers 1–13, resulting in 260 unique day-number combinations and yielding, for example, the day names One Alligator (*Ce Cipactli*), Five Snake (*Macuilli Coatl*) or Seven Flower (*Chicome Xochitl*). The calendar operated as a kind of astrological device; each unique day carried a load of good, bad or indifferent qualities. A knowledgeable *tonalpouhqui* (reader of the days) would be called upon to advise his client of the most auspicious days to undertake events such as a royal coronation, the onset of a war or the beginning of a large trading venture (Seven Snake was a particularly good day for this). Merchants displayed their considerable wares on the day Four Wind, embroiderers celebrated the day Seven Flower, dog breeders honoured the day Four Dog, and, as we have seen, slaves were eager for the onset of One Death, when they were to be treated especially well.

These are occasional or extraordinary events, but the calendar was also an integral element of the daily lives of all people. Every newborn child was given a name based on the day of his or her birth. A reader of the days was summoned to indicate or verify the day and advise the parents of the day's meaning for the child's future life. Some days foretold personalities: a One Deer person

Day Name	Meaning	Glyph	Associated Numbers			
cipactli	alligator		1	8	2	9
ehecatl	wind		2	9	3	10
calli	house		3	10	4	11
cuetzpallin	lizard		4	11	5	12
coatl	snake		5	12	6	13
miquiztli	death		6	13	7	1
mazatl	deer		7	1	8	2
tochtli	rabbit		8	2	9	3
atl	water		9	3	10	4
itzcuintli	dog		10	4	11	5
ozomatli	monkey		11	5	12	6
malinalli	grass		12	6	13	7
acatl	reed		13	7	1	8
ocelotl	jaguar		1	8	2	9
cuauhtli	eagle		2	9	3	10
cozcacuauhtli	vulture		3	10	4	11
ollin	movement		4	11	5	12
tecpatl	flint knife		5	12	6	13
quiahuitl	rain		6	13	7	1
xochitl	flower		7	1	8	2

The 260-day calendar.

would be timid and fearful, a Nine Alligator person would be hot-tempered and deceitful, and a Five Monkey person would be popular and friendly.

Beyond personality traits, did the day predict the child's future? Perhaps it was a fortuitous day such as Four Dog, which foretold of easy prosperity, or Ten Eagle with its promise of great bravery and courage. Or Eleven Vulture or Thirteen Rain, the bearer of which would grow old and satisfied. Or might it be an ill-fated day, such as One Jaguar with its foreboding misery, Two Rabbit with its burden of future drunkenness, One House with its addiction to gambling, or One Rain, the sign of sorcery and evil magic. Some days were ambiguous: a person born on Three Water could easily gain wealth, or as easily lose it. One Flower carried good fortune, but its namesake might be inclined to disregard its good graces and fall into 'rags and tatters'.[6]

While most of these prognostications sound definitive and either hopeful or hopeless, there was some wiggle room. A person could ruin even the most positive day sign with disreputable behaviour and irreverence towards the gods. On the other hand, a person could throw off at least some of the burden of a gloomy day sign by diligently following the 'exemplary life' and sincerely honouring the gods. So individuals did have some proactive input: their predicted futures could be circumvented, or at least muted. Additionally, alert parents had the option of waiting for up to four days before naming their child, thus mitigating the possible effects of an unfortunate birth-day name.

Whatever their actual life journeys, persons often assumed their birth-day sign as their personal name throughout their lives, supposedly also carrying the name's astrological baggage. Was Five Monkey always expected to be the life of the party, and One Deer a person to watch as a possible deserter on the battlefield? Unfortunately, we do not know to what extent people took these fateful predictions literally or found them to be self-fulfilling prophecies. In any event, people often ended up with other names during their lifetimes based on a physical or personality characteristic, a special life event or achievement (especially on the battlefield), or some poetic or even humiliating allusion. A courageous warrior might be named Tequani (Fierce Beast; lit. 'People Eater') or Ocelopan (Jaguar Banner); a woman might be affectionately named Miauaxiuitl (Turquoise Maize Flower) or Quiauhxochitl (Rain Flower). It was speculated that Motecuhzoma (Our Angry Lord) received his name from his scowling countenance during his naming ceremony.[7]

Many of these types of names persisted as surnames in colonial times, often in combination with a Christian name. So we find names such as Juan Tzonen (John Hairy), doña María Tonallaxochiatl (doña Mary Flowery Water of Summer), Magdalena Necahual (Magdalena Abandoned One), Martín Huitzilcoatl (Martín Hummingbird Snake), Gabriel Tomiquia (Gabriel the Death of Us) and Pedro Tochtli (Peter Rabbit).[8]

Determining a day name was but the beginning of a child's life. Enculturation into the 'exemplary life' and education into the skills of adulthood and an occupation followed in short order.

Socialization and Education

Society's rights and wrongs were instilled in Aztec children from a very early age. The *Codex Mendoza* offers us a year-by-year capsule of childhood socialization and punishments, from age three to age fourteen.[9] At each age, children are instructed or punished by a parent, boys by their fathers and girls by their mothers. Age three shows the children initially being advised by their parents, but at age four children are expected to help with light tasks, boys carrying water and girls being introduced to their lifelong work of spinning. The work increases from age five to seven: boys now carry heavier loads, help their fathers in the marketplace and learn how to fish in the lake; girls continue their instruction in spinning, gaining confidence.

At this point the document switches gears and presents punishments meted out to children who were obstinate, rebellious or did sloppy work. Parents were constantly admonishing their children (note the parents' speech scrolls), and corporal punishments became increasingly harsher with threats of pokes with maguey spines at age eight, actual piercing with the thorns at age nine, beating with a stick at age ten, and being held over a chilli fire at age eleven. At age twelve boys who were still intransigent were tied and laid out on damp ground; disobedient girls were required by their mothers to sweep during the night.

By age thirteen the girl seems to have straightened out and by then is sufficiently mature to undertake fundamental household tasks such as cooking and, at fourteen, weaving. Certainly she has been acquiring these skills all along, but by now she has mastered them. My ethnographic work with modern backstrap loom weavers in the Sierra Norte de Puebla reveals that girls begin learning to weave at age five and have mastered the skill by age fourteen: an impressive commitment by both the girl and her mother. Meanwhile, boys have grown enough to carry heavier loads, have learned to pole a canoe, and have advanced to fishing in the lake. At the same time the children are receiving essential training, they are also contributing to the economy and well-being of their households.

Of course these are broad generalizations, and not every parent or every child is alike. But it provides an idea of household education and the consequences of poor performance, whether in attitude, behaviour or quality of work. The girl's tasks are representative of just about any future work, although there would be nuances: a featherworker's daughter would learn to sort feathers by colour, a potter's daughter would learn to help with making pottery, or a high-ranking noble daughter may end up as a temple priestess or a royal wife. Others may learn special skills to become, for example, a midwife or a dye-maker. But whether noble or commoner, artisan or midwife, all women nonetheless learned to cook, spin, weave, tend children and in general manage a clean and orderly household.

Where boys are concerned, only a small fraction of the population were fishermen. We can take the *Codex Mendoza* to symbolize adult male activities in general, whether they be farming, crafting, trading or other occupations. It is doubtful that we would find noble boys undertaking tasks such as fishing.

In the *Codex Mendoza* boys entered a formal school setting at age fifteen, although other documents place children in local or priestly schools at age five, eight, ten, twelve or thirteen.[10] There were separate schools for noble and commoner boys. The noble school, or *calmecac*, perhaps accepted boys at a relatively early age, while the later ages may have been more appropriate for the *calpolli* schools, or *telpochcalli*.

Noble schools were attached to temples and were designed to train noble boys for elevated jobs in the state's administrative,

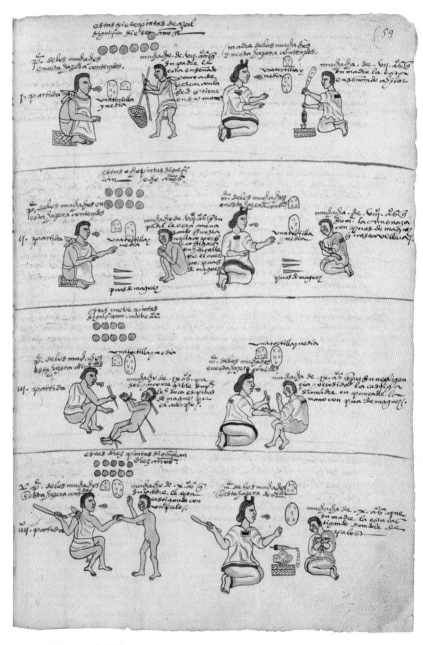

Socialization of children ages seven to ten.

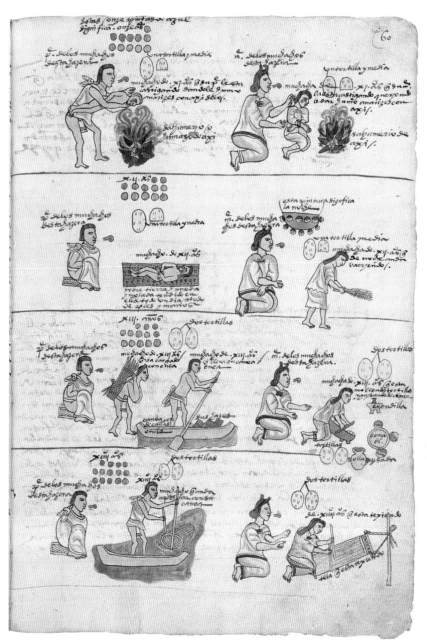

Socialization of children ages eleven to fourteen.

military and priestly hierarchies. Here they learned history, songs, calendrics, reading and writing, and the military arts. In addition to the fundamentals of fighting, these boys would have learned military strategies and tactics: if successful, they would be leaders on the battlefield and attend meetings in the war council chambers. Noble boys would also be eligible for governmental offices such as ambassadors, governors or tribute collectors, all lucrative and prestigious positions. Other options for boys trained in the *calmecac* were the priesthood and occupations such as teachers and scribes.

Telpochcalli education, in contrast, focused on military training for commoner boys. Since the Aztecs had no standing army, every man must be trained and available for service when called. A boy went to the school in his local *calpolli*, and also received some on-the-job training: 'they took him to the wars . . . And they taught him well how to guard himself with a shield; how one fought . . . they taught him well and made him see how he might take a captive.'[11] By the time he went to the wars, a man (whether farmer or potter) should be equipped, physically, materially and mentally, to meet his adversaries in open conflict.

A third school was the *cuicacalli* (house of song), attended by both boys and girls between the ages of twelve and fifteen. Since the purpose of this school was to teach the songs, dances and playing of musical instruments that were essential parts of the many public religious ceremonies, it is likely that this schooling was available to both nobles and commoners. The songs themselves instructed in and reinforced many of the fundamentals of Aztec religion such as stories of creation, the nature of the deities, the meaning of life and death, and the place of humans in an unstable universe.

Early socialization in the home and later education in formal schools provided children with the essential moral underpinnings, social understandings, ceremonial arts and practical skills needed for a proper and conforming adult life. It appears that most persons followed the 'exemplary life' as well as they could, but that does not mean that they did not stray occasionally, or that some people might not engage intentionally in deviance and crime.

Crime and Punishment

Wayward behaviour in the Aztec world ranged from minor moral infractions to major crimes threatening the stability of the social order, the city-state and even relations with the gods. Small malfeasances largely involved ignoring accepted virtues: we have seen that children were punished for obstreperous behaviour or sloppy work, and these deterrents continued into adult life. Many misbehaviours heavily impacted households: persistent troublemakers or quarrellers distressed others around them, an adulterer tore family members apart and drunkenness led to repeated disorderly conduct. Known troublemakers might be brought into line, especially by the women of the household, who were characterized as peacemakers. Barring that, they might leave their households and become vagabonds, potentially creating bigger problems for society at large.

Drunkenness was considered especially heinous. Perpetual drunks dishonoured their families and became poorer and poorer, possibly ending their lives in slavery. Excessive pulque-drinking was also believed to lead to adultery, an act particularly ruinous to household cohesion. And drunkenness and theft went hand-in-hand, as in the illustration on the following page, where an intoxicated man and woman break into a person's chest (and probably house) and steal its contents, including food and clothing. Theft ranged from petty acts (such as stealing from a neighbour's maize field) to marketplace thefts to thievery perpetrated through sorcery; this last was considered especially dangerous.

Drunkenness, theft and adultery were also considered to be offences at the city-state level, as were homicide, fraud, embezzlement, extortion, bribery and treachery or treason. All of these threatened the moral and social fabric of the society, and nibbled at the integrity of the social stratification system. Acts of homicide carried out by murderers, highwaymen or powerful evil sorcerers were considered violent and disruptive of orderly social life.[12] Fraud, embezzlement, extortion and bribery all violated the Aztec cardinal virtue of honesty. Fraud could involve the counterfeiting of cacao beans or falsifying marketplace measures, embezzlement and

An intoxicated couple take to thievery.

extortion might be attempted by ambitious tribute collectors, and unethical judges or attorneys might accept bribes. In each of these cases, the individual's occupation or social station offered opportunities for their specific crimes. As for treachery, traitors, informers and spies were an ever-present danger to any city-state's security. They were greatly feared and despised, although the Mexica also sent out their own spies (often as 'disguised' merchants) into enemy or rebellious regions where, it may be assumed, they were equally feared and despised.

Some locations were more vulnerable than others to criminal activity. Marketplaces, with their great quantities of material goods laid out in the open and enormous crowds milling about, were fertile grounds for thievery. The vendors were not only potential victims, however, but themselves had opportunities to overcharge, falsify measures and taint goods. Apparently they did – from bean vendors to the sellers of fine metal objects, each had specific ways of deceiving unsuspecting customers.[13] Elsewhere, thieves, murderers and highwaymen would have gravitated to isolated countryside locations. Beyond these, it must have been somewhat unnerving to know that anyone's home could be penetrated by powerful sorcerers who could stupefy the inhabitants or transform themselves into nefarious creatures, casually making off with all of the home's contents.

We do not know the extent or impact of deviance and crime in Aztec society. We do know that the Aztecs recognized these infractions and put in place a variety of informal and formal mechanisms to either deter such behaviours or directly deal with them after the fact.

Conformity was buttressed by the assumption that every properly enculturated Aztec knew the difference between right and wrong, and would be unlikely to engage in serious criminal behaviour (although virtually everyone at one time or another certainly fell short of the 'exemplary life', in whatever small ways). The Aztecs were not beyond shaming to enforce conformity, as in comparing an errant noble to a commoner, or a wayward Mexica to an ill-trained Otomí. Furthermore, specific religious ceremonies provided institutionalized settings for shaming, where young men who had not yet gained renown on the battlefield were openly taunted by young women – spurring them into valorous acts at the very next opportunity.[14]

These were social pressures, but the society also had a formal system of justice and attendant punishments for guilty perpetrators. We saw in the last chapter that there were separate courts for nobles and commoners; in either venue, procedures were strictly followed with oral and written testimonies included in the decisions. Judges were expected to be fair; if not, or if they were found guilty of other transgressions, they suffered severe penalties (this could be removal from office, or even execution). Like kings and other nobles, judges were often condemned more harshly than commoners for similar crimes: being nobles, they should know better. However, in a surprising show of leniency, judges convicted of bribery were warned for their first offence and shorn and removed from office for a second occurrence. Interestingly, this suggests repeated bribery-taking – perhaps it was fairly common.

With a guilty verdict, justice was swift and severe. Each crime carried its specific punishment. Many criminals faced execution: murderers, traitors, adulterers, extortionate tribute collectors, sellers of stolen goods, violators of sumptuary rules, persons moving field boundaries, and some thieves. Details of some of these executions are known: adulterers were usually stoned, traitors were dismembered, drunken nobles and priests were strangled, and thieves who stole farmers' crops had their heads crushed.

The justice system also exhibited some practical creativity: a man who committed a theft or a murder might be enslaved to his victim or victim's family in lieu of execution, thus replacing the loss. A person stealing food from temple or palace lands also met with enslavement (thus potentially increasing the labour pool of temples and palaces). The Aztecs' practical side has been seen throughout this book and leads us directly into the next chapter. What could be more practical than science, engineering, medicine and technical aspects of the material arts?

EIGHT

Science, Medicine and Life's Practicalities

> This tree [maguey] is so useful that they make wine, vinegar and syrup from it; also men and women's clothing and shoes, as well as cord, house beams, roof tiles, needles for sewing and for stitching wounds and other things. In addition they gather the leaves of this tree or teasel which they cultivate like we do vineyards and which they call maguey, and they put these leaves to cook in underground ovens. Then they crush the cooked leaves with a wooden instrument, removing the peels or roots, and they drink so much of this liquor that they get drunk.[1]

The Aztecs were a practical people, and a paramount symbol of Aztec practicality was the multipurpose maguey plant. Maguey is abundant in central Mexico, normally growing at elevations of around 1,800 metres (*c.* 5,400 ft) and above. It is capable of growing on thin soils and in relatively cold and dry environments, and is resistant to frost, storms and hail. In addition to its many uses, its role in extending human cultivation into ecological zones incapable of supporting other crops, such as maize and beans, cannot be understated. Maguey was also interplanted with these seasonal crops (on better soils) and its production was year-round (although sap extraction tended to occur in the autumn and early winter, 'off' times in the cycles of most other crops). Maguey is hardy and along with the similarly hardy prickly pear cactus helped sustain populations for centuries past (and to the present day), especially in times of drought.

A maguey (agave) plant.

The Aztecs and their neighbours and predecessors used maguey plants in numerous practical and creative ways. The plants themselves fenced house plots and fields and terraced hillside plots (inhibiting erosion and conserving soil). And I have observed women, having washed their clothing in a stream, drying those garments on the leaves of streamside maguey plants.

Other important uses included the extraction of fibres for cordage, nets and woven clothing; the small, inner leaves were silky-textured, while the larger, outer leaves yielded coarser fibres. Careful separation of the fibres, leaving one fibre attached to a leaf's sharp thorn, provided the weaver with a handy needle and thread. Fibres were softened and pounded into paper. The leaves also had (and still have) a medical value: they contain a sap that serves as an antiseptic. The needles had a multitude of uses, including punishments, stitching wounds and ritual bloodletting. Leaves, hearts and stalks were also prepared and cooked as important sources of food. Different parts of the plant had almost endless additional uses: sandals, construction materials, household utensils and surfaces for making featherwork designs; even a beehive could be formed from an exhausted core. When a plant died its remains were used for fuel. Nothing went to waste.

The liquid sap was particularly important. It was (and still is) derived from the core of mature plants; it is estimated that only about 2 to 7 per cent of plants in a region are productive for this purpose at any one time.[2] A plant exudes sap for three to six months, after which it dies and must be replaced by a new one, when the lengthy growth cycle is repeated. During its sap-producing phase the farmer stimulates the production of sap by scraping the sides of the open core and collecting the accumulated sap. A conscientious farmer does this every day. Meanwhile, all the other plants must be tended as they grow to maturity.[3]

The sap, as an important nutritional component in the Aztec diet,[4] was consumed as a sweet honey called *aguamiel* ('honey water', unfermented maguey sap), prepared as *pulque*, turned into a thick syrup or solid sugar 'cakes', and concocted into medicines.

The sap spoils quickly, so maguey cultivation and *aguamiel/pulque* production usually took place in close proximity to the planted fields. *Aguamiel* and *pulque* must be consumed in only about one week, so the producers must rely on well-honed techniques and well-established distribution channels, especially local markets. Solid sugar, on the other hand, could be stored for months. Cultural restrictions on the consumption of *pulque* must be kept in mind; because drunkenness was a serious offence, imbibing this fermented beverage was largely restricted to ritual settings and to the elderly. Its intoxicating strength could be enhanced with the addition of a root that gave the brew an added kick. The *pulque* producers knew this well.

The Aztecs employed observation, empiricism and experimentation in exploiting maguey and other resources. A goal of this chapter is to emphasize the Aztecs' impressive knowledge base in a selection of scientific arenas: natural history, representational art, astronomy and medicine. And being a practical people, they not only accumulated vast funds of knowledge, but applied the knowledge to activities such as food production and preparation, engineering, architecture, material technologies and curing.

Natural History and Representational Art

The Aztecs were keenly aware of the environment of which they were a part: they labelled and classified natural features, fauna and flora, and observed characteristics, behaviours and rhythms of the creatures around them. They understood ecological processes and their consequences and involved themselves in transforming their environment. In their understanding of the natural world, the Aztecs combined their hunter-gatherer background with agrarian and urban experiences.

Landscape features, especially mountains and water sources, were noted for both their practical importance and their religious significance, and were even embedded in the Aztec political structure. A city-state was an *altepetl*, or water-mountain (*atl* = water, *tepetl* = hill or mountain), highlighting the essentials of life. Mountains were considered sources of water: in a practical sense, rain-bearing clouds accumulated over mountains; in a religious sense, minions of the rain god Tlaloc resided in mountains, pouring out their jugs of water for human benefit. The Aztecs understood specific attributes and qualities of different types and sources of water and treated them accordingly: springs provided sweet water, raging rivers could drown people, and a whirlpool near Tenochtitlan was fearsome enough to require periodic offerings.

The extent of empirical observations conducted by the Aztecs and generations of their ancestors is reflected in their impressive knowledge of their natural world. This is especially reflected in the attributes and behaviours of animals: they recognized that the opossum's fur colour changed with age, that locusts reproduced underground, and that hummingbirds became dormant as temperatures changed. Characteristics of animals and plants were important enough to be often embedded in the people's metaphors, adages, omens and riddles. For example, a poor person was likened to a humble turtle dove, a fugitive resembled a deer or rabbit, and a great ruler protected his people like an overarching cypress or silk cotton tree. If a rabbit entered one's house, it foretold the loss of the house or the householder; even more seriously, if a skunk appeared in a house, the resident would die. Riddles posed easy questions to any Aztec, who would also know the obvious answers: 'What is it that is a small blue gourd bowl filled with popcorn?' (the heavens); 'What is a small white stone holding a quetzal feather?' (an onion); 'What is that which is a stone of red ochre which goes jumping?' (a flea).[5] Furthermore, we have already seen that many of the day names in the 260-day calendar were animals (jaguar, deer, rabbit, monkey, eagle, vulture and so on), and to some extent the days carried attributes associated with those animals: people with deer or rabbit names will flee in fear, those with a jaguar name behaved in warfare as fierce beasts, and those with a monkey name will be lively and fun. On a grander plane, many deities carried animal and plant associations. Examples are Huitzilopochtli (Hummingbird-on-the-left), Xochiquetzal (Flower-quetzal bird) and Cihuacoatl (Woman-serpent). Nature was an integral part of the people's world view as well as their daily actions.

Aztecs were active participants in ecological dynamics. While they believed they were a part of (not apart from) the rest of nature around them, they also understood that they had the capability to transform their world. They viewed it as a place of instability, and their signal role as actors revolved around maintaining harmony. When the system went awry, they were responsible for restoring balance. Rulers were particularly well situated to make an impact on their natural world. They orchestrated waterworks such as dykes, aqueducts and dams to control that essential resource. Motecuhzoma Xocoyotzin (at least) established a splendid zoo and aviary at his palace. Matthew Restall concludes that this ruler was a 'collector imperial and extraordinaire . . . collecting was at the very heart of his identity as emperor'.[6]

Motecuhzoma's zoo and aviary (*totocalli*, 'bird house') were also the domain of the palace artisans, who had access to the feathers, hides and other animal resources for their crafts. Andrés de Tapia, a Spanish conquistador who visited Motecuhzoma's palace before its destruction, later recalled seeing lions, tigers, wolves, foxes, falcons, hawks, snakes and other vipers in pottery vessels, and waterfowl. He writes that six hundred men were employed in the care of the birds, and that there was a place set aside 'where the sick birds could be cured'.[7] This last detail suggests not only that they cared deeply for their avians, but that they had acquired skills for restoring their health.

Kings (and probably other lords) combined their pleasure gardens with plant science. We do not know how much scientific information was acquired as knowledge for knowledge's sake, how much was sought for practical purposes, and how much to satisfy rulers' vanities. Two of the most famous botanical gardens were at Huaxtepec and Tetzcotzinco. The spectacular garden at Huaxtepec was created by Motecuhzoma Ilhuicamina in warm lands that he had conquered just south of the Basin of Mexico. This lush place had convenient springs that could be dammed to make a watery paradise. To establish his botanical garden around this water feature, he ordered that exotic lowland flora, including cacao trees and a great variety of plants with aromatic flowers, be brought to Huaxtepec from another conquered province, Cuetlaxtlan on the Gulf Coast. The plants arrived quickly (befitting a royal order), their roots encased in soil and wrapped in cloths, and were attended by knowledgeable gardeners who stayed with their floral charges in the Huaxtepec garden to assure their successful growth.[8] Reportedly the experiment was a success on two levels: the plants thrived beyond their expectations, and Motecuhzoma achieved his glorified legacy. This garden continued in use throughout the rule of the second Motecuhzoma, containing ornamental plants and medicinal trees at that time. The rulers of Texcoco had an expansive botanical garden at Tetzcotzinco, near Texcoco: this was a hill with magnificent water features (including a royal stone bath), religious monuments and an array of exotic plants, including those with useful medicinal properties. In this royal garden the Texcocan king cultivated plants brought there from throughout his realm.

Nature was brought into cities in the form of palatial gardens, zoos and aviaries – and representational art. Aztec artists were masters of this genre in whatever medium: stone sculpture, metalwork, featherwork, woodwork, ceramics, stone mosaics and painting (and combinations of these). Some of their most popular subjects were animals and plants. Serpents, jaguars, coyotes and dogs were commonly sculpted in stone, along with many other creatures: monkeys, rabbits, eagles, frogs and even the lowly grasshopper and

A sitting monkey sculpted from volcanic rock.

flea. Animals and plants cast in metals (especially gold and silver) included jaguars, monkeys, fish, birds, butterflies, snakes, lizards, flowers and ears of corn. Featherwork, woodwork, pottery and stone mosaic work likewise used nature as primary subjects (recall the feathered coyote shield). Animals and plants also frequently appear in paintings, as in the initial page of the *Codex Mendoza* with its central figure of an eagle on a cactus; local plants; plants, an animal, and a bird in personal names; and rabbit heads in every fourth year-name.

In all these media living things were depicted realistically, with artists attending carefully even to textures of furs and feathers. Reportedly Motechuzoma Xocoyotzin ordered that replicas of all the plants and animals in his known world be created from metals and feathers, and displayed in his zoo. Similarly, the Texcocan king had images in gold and stone mosaic work made of 'every bird, fish, or animal which could not be obtained alive'.[9] One cannot resist the conclusion that the kings from these most powerful city-states had entered into a sort of natural history competition, with actual gardens and with artificial depictions of nature.

Not only did artists depict living things with meticulous natural accuracy, they also conveyed their vitality. In his pose and demeanour, the sculpted monkey pictured here, while sitting, appears ready to engage with his viewer. Rattlesnakes are poised to strike, frogs are crouching and birds are perched or in flight. Reportedly metalsmiths fashioned a fish with one fin of gold and the other of silver, and another fish with alternating scales of gold and silver. Artists were also adept at including actual movements in their creations: a skilled artist created a golden parrot whose tongue, head and wings could all move; another made a coiled snake with a movable tail; and yet another created a monkey 'which moves its head, tongue, hands and feet, and in its hands they put little implements, so that the figure seems to be dancing with them'.[10] This is dynamic art, the artists cleverly representing living nature.

Astronomy, Time and the Solar Calendar

The Aztecs were astute observers of the heavens. They drew on their predecessors' fount of knowledge based on millennia of celestial observations. These included the movements of the sun and moon, the repeated appearance of comets, the scheduling of lunar and solar eclipses, and the appearance of meteor showers. These celestial observations allowed the astronomers to calculate the lengths of the lunar month and the solar year, and the synodic period of Venus (584 days). They were also interested in pinpointing the solstices and equinoxes on natural and built landscapes.

While empirical observations and calculations provided a scientific base for their understanding of the extraterrestrial realms, the people also projected their own cultural conceptions on the heavens in the form of constellations: our familiar Plough, or Big Dipper, was seen as their Tezcatlipoca (a war god), our Pleiades was their 'Marketplace', and they saw part of our Taurus as a 'Fire Drill'.[11] In a similar vein, while we perceive a man in the moon, they see a rabbit. This last image is directly connected to their mythologies: during the creation of the present world the gods hurled a rabbit onto that celestial body to dim it. Anyone seeing the rabbit in the moon would be reminded of this important myth.

Lacking visual pollution such as electric lighting and smog, ancient peoples were accustomed to clearly viewing the heavens, night after night, year after year. It is not a stretch to suggest that their repeated observations led to sound calculations of the movements of heavenly bodies. The Aztecs undoubtedly inherited much of their astronomical knowledge. But they did not rest on that inheritance; rather, they were curious and interested in pursuing astronomical observations. The Texcocan ruler Nezahualpilli (r. 1472–1515) was an avid astronomer:

> It is said that he was a great astrologer; that he was much concerned with understanding the movement of the celestial bodies . . . he would seek in his kingdoms for those who knew of such things, and he would bring them to his court . . . and

he would go on the roof of his palace, and from there he would watch the stars, and he would discuss problems with them.[12]

While farmers and other commoners would have a working knowledge of the movements of celestial bodies in the cosmos, it was the elite who had the tools and time to conduct detailed studies. On palace roofs and atop tall temples, rulers and priests could devote long night-time hours to naked-eye observations as the heavens unfolded above them, aided by crossed sticks for lines of sight or a device containing small holes to enhance their view.

The Aztecs and their ancestors and neighbours embedded their precise astronomical observations into calculations of time. The 260-day astrological calendar approximates the human gestation period, is somewhat more distantly related to the average interval of the appearance of Venus as evening or morning star, and is more closely tied to Mesoamerica's agricultural cycle.[13]

More obviously practical was the solar calendar of 365 days. It combined twenty months of eighteen days each (making 360 days), with five fickle days at the end. The solar year is more precisely 365.2422 days long, and we do not know how the Aztecs corrected the inevitable calendrical slippage from natural seasonal cycles, as we do with leap years. Each month was overseen by a major deity and celebrated with specific public ceremonies; since many of those ceremonies addressed rain, fertility or other matters of seasonal importance, it was important that the calendar and seasons synchronize. In addition to these religious associations, the solar calendar was also used to schedule large and small markets at daily, five-day or twenty-day intervals.

This 365-day calendar was meshed with the 260-day calendar to yield 18,980 unique days, the equivalent of 52 solar years. For instance, Tenochtitlan fell to the Spaniards and their indigenous allies on 13 August 1521 according to the Spanish (Julian) calendar. In the Aztec calendar, this was the date Ome Xocotl uetzi Ce Coatl (Two Xocotl uetzi, One Snake), the second day of the tenth month in the solar calendar combined with the day One Snake in the astrological calendar. Each of the 52 years was designated by a year name (House, Rabbit, Reed and Flint Knife), and each of the names was attached to the numbers 1–13 (thus 4 × 13 = 52). While the significance of this more encompassing 'calendar round' was primarily religious, these year counts were also used to record historical events. Looking back at the *Codex Mendoza*'s initial page, we can trace the events of Tenochtitlan's early history from Two House (upper left) to Three Rabbit, Four Reed and Five Flint Knife, on through the New Fire Ceremony on Two Reed, and around the page's periphery to Thirteen Reed. The Aztecs' intertwined calendrical system served to order their temporal world, past and present, mundane and monumental.

Medicine

During their lifetimes Aztec people almost inevitably faced illnesses and suffered injuries. Children were especially vulnerable to dysentery and diarrhoea, and we know from skeletal remains that some experienced iron-deficiency anaemia (probably caused by dietary deficiencies or intestinal parasites). Some children had dental issues, likely from poor hygiene or infections. Around the ages of 30 to 35, some adults suffered arthritis, rheumatism or tuberculosis,

A sweatbath.

with dental problems continuing. Young women faced the hazards and uncertainties of childbirth. And the skulls and limbs of adult men reveal fractures, dislocations and infected wounds – this was, after all, a militaristic society. Highland peoples tended to be susceptible to respiratory and gastrointestinal ailments, while lowlanders were more likely to host parasites.[14] The fortunate individual who survived these dangers and afflictions could expect to live a long life; people reaching the age of seventy were rewarded with the right to drink *pulque* at will, attended by their obedient children and grandchildren.[15]

Medical matters were in the hands of trained physicians and midwives. These knowledgeable specialists had at their disposal a wide range of remedies to relieve ailments, cure diseases and patch up injuries. Physicians (men and women) were experts at diagnosing problems and settling on appropriate remedies to restore their patients' health. We do not know if physicians went to war to come to the aid of battlefield casualties, much as do modern military medics. I think it is safe to assume that they did, since battlefield wounds from piercing, slashing and bashing were often severe and would have required immediate attention. The scientific basis for the physician's craft appears in this statement of his or her responsibilities: 'The good physician is . . . a knower of herbs, of stones, of trees, of roots. He has (results of) examinations, experience, prudence.'[16] In contrast, as one might imagine, the bad physician only made his or her patients worse, defrauded them, or even bewitched or killed them.

Childbirth was the special province of midwives who cared for women before, during and after childbirth. In the months prior to birth, the midwife offered sage advice to the expectant mother. She might counsel the woman against napping during the day lest her child be born with 'abnormally large eyelids', or warn her that relaxing in an overly hot sweatbath would cause the baby to overheat and get stuck. Eating chalk or earth would result in a sickly child.[17] Unpleasant scenarios. But it was not all negative. The midwife imparted practical positive advice reflecting her familiarity with the woman's condition: eat well and do only light tasks. The midwife's duties were quintessentially practical: she massaged the mother's growing belly, positioned the baby, oversaw the mother's frequent sweatbath sessions, and used curative herbs and other natural materials to ease and protect both mother and child. An adept and well-trained midwife, assisting with the birth itself, must always be prepared for possible complications. In cases of emergency, she had in her medical arsenal both practical remedies and appeals to the gods.[18]

Good health began with preventive measures. Among the most important of these were an adequate diet and good hygiene. While the Aztec diet usually provided balanced nutrients, the Aztec domain periodically experienced famines, and not all individuals on the social ladder had equal access to sufficient food or a regularly nutritious diet. Malnutrition did occur. The Aztecs valued cleanliness and bathed often, had access to clean drinking water, and managed effective waste disposal. But physical remains indicate that they sometimes fell short of their own ideals: this is seen in dental remains that reveal cavities and tartar, even though the Aztecs had very specific dental cleaning techniques that included washing (with urine, salt, chillies and other materials), rubbing (with charcoal, ashes and honey), scraping and chewing gum. Other preventive measures targeted special conditions: a nursing mother was told to avoid eating avocados, otherwise her infant would become ill; a heavy eater, at the end of an enjoyable feast, smoked tobacco as a digestive aid; and an eager warrior charged into battle protected with upper body armour and a shield.

When preventive measures failed, as we have seen they could, cures were enlisted. A proper cure required a sound diagnosis, if possible made by a skilled physician. Physicians based their diagnoses and curative solutions on training, experience and available remedies (especially from plants); it was largely an empirical undertaking. Their knowledge was impressive and must have been developed from countless observations and experiments over millennia. Their extensive pharmacopoeia dealt with issues as varied as headaches, stomach aches, coughs, fevers, parasites, skin sores, insomnia and unstable mental states. They could treat snakebites (with tobacco), a broken skull (with maguey sap), and a severed nose (with salt and bee honey). These examples are quite straightforward, but many cures involved combinations of several different natural materials: arriving at the correct formula must have involved considerable trial and error, persistence and perhaps some good luck. The efficacy of these and countless other cures is evidenced scientifically: in one study, 85 per cent of 118 plants ethnohistorically identified with curative properties were found to be effective in modern medical terms. For instance, hot maguey sap was applied to wounds (especially if they became infected), and the sap is known today to effectively inhibit the growth of bacteria on wounded flesh. Without the concept of bacteria at hand, the Aztecs could not phrase this cure in those terms, but their experience taught them that it worked.

Aztec medicine was an empirical and applied science. That said, all aspects of this enterprise contained spiritual components as well. Since the gods could visit unpleasant diseases and deformities on disrespectful individuals, it behoved people to properly observe godly rituals. In another vein, a vengeful person might employ a sorcerer to visit an unsavoury malady on his or her enemy. Given multiple sources of illnesses (gods, sorcerers or natural causes), medical practitioners were armed with ritual as well as practical tools in effecting their cures. In addition, midwives not only assisted in physical matters but were responsible for ritual activities surrounding the birth of the child. People's well-being was complex and unpredictable, and medical practitioners, as well as their patients, left no stone unturned in seeking healthy lives.

While the Aztecs and their neighbours suffered from numerous ailments and illnesses, they did not have to cope with massive epidemics such as smallpox, measles or influenza until their contact with the Spaniards in the early sixteenth century. However, with no immunities to these foreign diseases, the native population suffered in the extreme, as we shall see.

Applications of Aztec Scientific Inquiry

This vast fund of accumulated knowledge had practical applications for the Aztecs and their neighbours. This included understanding the anatomy, behaviour, life cycles and ecology of wild animals and plants. For instance, the night-time song of the American bittern heralded heavy rains. More specifically, the evening antics of the ruddy duck predicted rain at dawn and another bird's song warned of imminent frost. Listening to nature provided the Aztecs with some measure of predictability in an uncertain world. They were also aware of the rarity of certain creatures, such as the wood ibis: catching it was a bad omen, and few people would challenge omens. Rulers' botanical gardens and zoos served to conserve multitudes of species, whether intended to do so or not. Conservation is at least implied.

The Aztecs sought to control their environment and secure a steadfast place in that world. Primary among these strategies were sophisticated agricultural techniques, including intercropping, terracing, irrigation and *chinampas*. We should not minimize the impact of generations upon generations of farmers as 'silent biologists', especially in hybridizing plants and improving agricultural techniques, thereby expanding the food supply. The Aztecs used complicated food-processing technologies, including mixing lime with maize and fermenting maguey sap.

Aztecs excelled in managing water through dykes, dams and aqueducts. They appear to have been mostly successful, but there were unintended consequences to some human meddling. We are reminded of Ahuitzotl's poorly conceived aqueduct that visited a devastating flood on Tenochtitlan. Ahuitzotl also was responsible for bringing great-tailed grackles to Tenochtitlan from the coast and ordering their protection. However, unforeseen by him, these birds became so prolific that they shortly turned into a burden on the highland ecosystem.

The Aztecs were masters of transforming natural materials into usable products and objects. These complex technologies included the production of bronze through exact combinations of copper, tin and arsenic; the creation of exceptionally bouncy rubber balls by combining latex with juice from morning glory vines; the manufacture of a lime plaster that is still hard as concrete; and the concoction of recipes for formulating and fixing stable and long-lasting paints and dyes. The list goes on and on. It should be emphasized that the Aztecs adopted most of these technologies from their ancestors or neighbours (for instance, bronze from the Tarascans to the west).

Practical applications of astronomy primarily involved the ordering of time through calendars and the alignments of major buildings, most notably temples. A prime example is Tenochtitlan's Great Temple, which was aligned so that the rising sun at the equinoxes rose precisely between the twin sanctuaries of Huitzilopochtli and Tlaloc. During one temple expansion, the sanctuaries were incorrectly aligned and the ruler had the structure torn down and put to rights, suggesting the great importance of this alignment.

All of this was embedded in a cultural world view that emphasized balance and harmony in all aspects of the natural and supernatural worlds. While we may separate natural from supernatural, there is no evidence that the Aztecs did so. On the contrary, their natural world carried deep symbolic, religious and ritual meanings. While celestial observations were empirical and observation devices were clever, astronomy for the Aztecs extended beyond their practical utility. Animals and plants were essential for human life, but also served as metaphors for life's values and were front and centre in gods' identities and ritual activities: quail were frequently sacrificed and animals such as jaguars, serpents, eagles and canines were ritually buried in Tenochtitlan's sacred precinct.[19] Landscape features, especially mountains and water, were religiously important: mountains were simultaneously the home of maize, water and the gods. Diseases were diagnosed and treated with both natural and supernatural techniques. This vibrant world of the supernatural is pursued in the next chapter.

NINE

GODS, SACRIFICE AND THE MEANING OF LIFE

Following the creation of the Fifth Sun (the current age),

> Then [the god] Quetzalcoatl went to the dead land, and when he came to the dead land lord, the dead lord lady, he said to him, 'I've come for the precious bones that you are keeping. I've come to get them.'
>
> Then he said, 'To do what, Quetzalcoatl?'
>
> And he answered him, 'It's because the gods are sad. Who will there be on earth?'
>
> The dead land lord replied, 'Very well. Blow my conch horn and circle four times around my precious realm.' But his conch horn was not hollow.
>
> Then he summoned worms, who hollowed it out. Then bumblebees and honeybees went in. Then he blew on it, and the dead land lord heard him.

After some to-and-fro,

> Then [Quetzalcoatl] takes the precious bones. The male bones are in one pile, the female bones are in another pile. Then Quetzalcoatl takes them, wraps them up, and comes carrying them off.
>
> Again, the dead land lord said to his messengers, 'Spirits, Quetzalcoatl is really taking the precious bones away. Spirits, go dig him a pit.' Then they went and dug it for him.

So he fell into the pit, stumbled and fell, and quail frightened him and he lost consciousness.

Then he spilled the precious bones, and the quail bit into them, nibbled them.

When Quetzalcoatl arose, he gathered up the bones and took them to Tamoanchan where a goddess ground them up and Quetzalcoatl bled himself, dripping his blood on the pulverized bones. 'Then all the gods . . . did penance . . . Then they said, "Holy ones, humans, have been born." It's because they did penance for us.'[1]

Quetzalcoatl (Feathered Serpent) was one of Mesoamerica's most revered deities. He had deep roots in ancient Mesoamerican civilizations and appears to have enjoyed almost universal appeal. Perhaps one reason for his popularity lay in the multiple roles he filled: he was a primary creator god, assured that humans inhabited the earth (as seen above), was the patron of rulership and a god of priests, oversaw the luxury artisans and the priestly schools, and was the good wind that preceded the rains. He was the morning star, he invented the calendar, and by various accounts he also acquired maize, *pulque* and music with which to honour the gods. He was also associated with a great legendary culture hero of Tula, Topiltzin Quetzalcoatl. He was especially worshipped by merchants at Cholula, a famed pilgrimage destination for people travelling great distances and wishing to personally honour Quetzalcoatl.

The wind god, Ehecatl-Quetzalcoatl, is depicted in the *Codex Magliabechiano*. One hallmark of this god is his jaguar-skin conical headgear; in this image a bone is attached to his cap, and several duck feathers, two flowers and a sipping hummingbird dangle from the bone. He is also identifiable here by his protruding red mask, probably associated with a duck bill, through which he blew the wind; his shell necklace and conch shell breast ornament; and the curved inlaid spear thrower he wields.

The *Codex Magliabechiano* is so named because it was found in the vast library of the eccentric but respected Italian scholar and bibliophile Antonio Magliabechi (1633–1714). The codex is a colonial pictorial manuscript composed on European paper in the mid-sixteenth century by native artists in pre-conquest style. Its

The god Ehecatl-Quetzalcoatl.

early history is shadowy, but we understand that it was copied from a now-lost prototype drawn by a well-trained native artist between 1529 and 1553. Other copies of this prototype were also made, but the *Magliabechiano* is considered the most accurate existing version. The artist who drew this figure was an accomplished copyist and clearly familiar with complex pre-Columbian religious iconography and symbolism. Several other paintings of this deity exist (in this document and others), and while there are variations, some standard motifs always appear: his conical head gear, his conch shell adornment and his facial protruding beak or mask. Beyond these essential elements, he may wear variable back devices, carry differently designed shields, wield dissimilar spear throwers or hold a priestly bag. He was also sculpted in stone as a serpent wrapped in graceful feathers. These variations should come as no surprise, given the diversity of Quetzalcoatl's guises, the range of his responsibilities and his popularity across ethnic groups.

Quetzalcoatl was one god in a large pantheon of deities. They were embedded in a complex religious system that also included myths relating cosmic stories, a hierarchical universe with its sacred landscapes, numerous and imposing temples with their priests and priestesses, and flamboyant ceremonies, some of which included human sacrifice.[2]

Stories of the Universe: Myths

The Aztec cosmic universe was a potent and dynamic place: 'it had a tumultuous past, an unstable present, and an uncertain future.'[3] Its past and the role of humans in its present and future were wrapped in a large repertoire of colourful myths. These myths narrated cycles of cosmic creation and destruction, related the feats and failures of powerful gods and goddesses, spoke of sacrifices and glorified culture heroes. Myths were vivid, dramatic, and must have been riveting in their telling. Many of these myths have variant (mostly regional) versions; the four recounted here are typical of their genre.

On a grand scale, the Aztecs believed that the universe had been created five times, four of them ending in destruction. Each age was named for the day of its cataclysmic destruction, was inhabited by specific types of humans and was presided over by its own powerful deity. The first age, Nahui Ocelotl (Four Jaguar), was overseen by Tezcatlipoca and populated by giants who subsisted on acorns and at the end of the age were eaten by jaguars. Then Nahui Ehecatl (Four Wind) took over and was ruled by Quetzalcoatl, who oversaw humans living on piñon nuts. This age was destroyed by hurricanes and the humans were transformed into monkeys. The third age, Nahui Quiahuitl (Four Rain), was the charge of Tlaloc (rain god), who cared for humans who subsisted on an aquatic seed. A fiery rain (probably a volcanic eruption) abruptly ended this age, with humans being changed into dogs, turkeys and butterflies. Nahui Atl (Four Water) then arrived as the fourth age, ruled by Chalchiuhtlicue (a water goddess), who presided over humans living on wild seeds (perhaps the ancestor of maize). These humans were transformed into fish in a great flood.

The fifth and current age, Nahui Ollin (Four Movement), was ruled by the sun god Tonatiuh, who oversaw humans subsisting on maize. The Aztecs lived in this age. They believed in the four ages that had come and gone before them, and that their age had an uncertain future. It was destined to be destroyed by earthquakes in a time when people would be devoured by celestial monsters. According to their calendar, this cataclysm would occur at the end of a 52-year cycle.

The creation of this fifth age is recounted in especially vivid and epic narratives. The story goes like this. At the end of the fourth age, all fell into darkness. In this cosmic void, the gods assembled at Teotihuacan, where they agreed that one of them must leap into a fire to create the new sun. Two gods volunteered: the arrogant Tecuciztecatl and the humble and unimpressive Nanahuatzin. Both gods ritually prepared themselves, but in the end Tecuciztecatl faltered and failed in his task – he tried and tried to jump into the fire, but each time his courage abandoned him. Seeing this, Nanahuatzin took a great leap into the fire, finally followed by a humiliated Tecuciztecatl and an eagle and a jaguar (explaining the black marks on both creatures). But still, all was dark. Then the gods saw a light slowly rise in the east – the new sun, as Nanahuatzin, was born and slowly rising in the sky, providing heat and light to the world. Before the gods could rejoice, a second sun arose as Tecuciztecatl also appeared in the sky. To their horror, the gods realized that two suns would scorch and destroy the earth. To solve this problem, one of the gods seized a rabbit and flung it into the second sun, dimming its surface and creating the moon. This is the rabbit that the Aztecs saw on the surface of the full moon. All seemed well, but this was not the end to their godly problems: as it happened, both sun and moon stopped dead in the sky. To energize them, Ehecatl (Quetzalcoatl) slew all the gods present as a sacrifice. But still the stubborn celestial bodies did not budge until Ehecatl set them in motion with his mighty wind. Quetzalcoatl, as recounted at the beginning of this chapter, was also instrumental in creating humans to inhabit this fifth world.

Another myth, set in historic times, had the effect of humanizing the gods. In this story the high priests (or gods) Tezcatlipoca and Topiltzin Quetzalcoatl resided (perhaps co-ruling) in the legendary and idealized Tula of the Toltecs. As a priest, Quetzalcoatl was held up as a model of religious piety and devotion. Yet when he became ill, his arch-rival Tezcatlipoca (a warlike wizard god) tricked him into imbibing *pulque* and becoming drunk (a violation of Quetzalcoatl's priestly vows), leading him to commit incest with his sister (who was also drunk by then). Waking up to intense remorse and humiliation, Quetzalcoatl left Tula and headed off to the Gulf coast with a small band of followers where, depending on the account, he rose into the heavens, journeyed to the east or disappeared.

Close to the hearts of the Mexica was the myth recounting the birth of their patron god, Huitzilopochtli (Hummingbird-on-the-left). As his mother Coatlicue (an earth-mother goddess) was sweeping one day, she picked up a ball of feathers and put it in her belt. Soon after, she realized she was pregnant, much to the fury of her daughter Coyolxauhqui (the moon) and her numerous sons, the Centzon Huitznahua or four hundred stars of the southern hemisphere.[4] At a mountain called Coatepec (Snake Mountain) they attacked their pregnant mother in a furious rage, intending to kill her. At the last moment, with tension mounting, Huitzilopochtli emerged fully formed and armed with a potent fire serpent. He saved his mother by vigorously fighting off his half-siblings, dismembering Coyolxauhqui and dispersing the others. This myth has its corollary in legendary-historical accounts. On their long journey to central Mexico, the Mexica dealt with internal factions, and a memorable quarrel occurred between Huitzilopochtli and his sister Malinalxochitl. Huitzilopochtli prevailed, and his sister took her faction elsewhere, settling at Malinalco.[5] The parallel between this story and the mythical birth of their patron god was not lost on the Mexica. Neither was the supernatural message of the myth: Huitzilopochtli was the sun and his enemies were deities of the night. To bring heat and sunlight daily, and fight off the darkness, he must receive energy from his worshippers, which they supplied in the form of blood sacrifices. This weighty responsibility fell on the Mexica, who had carried Huitzilopochtli in their long migration to Tenochtitlan.

The goddess Coyolxauhqui dismembered by her brother Huitzilopochtli.

Myths explained, taught and entertained. The telling of these stories must have captivated the rapt audiences. Repeated and reinforced on the public ceremonial stage, they imparted moral imperatives to the faithful. They also validated religious beliefs and practices, many of which re-enacted or at least addressed the primary message of the myth. For instance, re-enacting the birth of Huitzilopochtli, human sacrifices ended up at the foot of the Great Temple (itself called Coatepec), where a monumental sculpture of a dismembered Coyolxauhqui lay. In another case, the Aztecs were keenly aware of their impending cosmic doom, with the fate of four previous worlds in mind. To stave off this unpleasant fate, the Aztecs performed a New Fire ceremony at the end of every 52-year cycle when they were most vulnerable. This was an especially significant myth and ceremony for every Aztec. The gods had made sacrifices for humanity, leaving people in perpetual debt to them. This debt must be paid over and over again through ritual blood sacrifices. On a more mundane level, the tale of Tezcatlipoca and Quetzalcoatl is almost folkloric, reminding people of the evils of drunkenness and bad behaviour.

The Aztec Universe and Sacred Landscapes

Myths also explained the structure of the universe and the place of humans within that universe. The world narrated by these stories was divided into a hierarchical arrangement of thirteen layers in the heavens, nine layers in the underworld and an intermediate terrestrial layer, the habitable world of the Aztecs. This terrestrial plane counted as the first layer in both the upper and lower domains.

Some of the twelve cosmic layers above the earth's surface were characterized by recognizable celestial bodies (such as the sun, moon, comets, the many stars and the Milky Way), which were also considered divine. For instance, the sun and moon were constituted as deities, and the stars were the Centzon Huitznahua who attacked Huitzilopochtli's mother in the myth recounted above. Other layers featured strictly supernatural occupants, such as fire serpents and female celestial monsters. A specific god presided over every tier. Each level also featured its own celestial bird such as the hummingbird, quail, barn owl, turkey, macaw or quetzal; one of the layers featured a butterfly. At the very top, remote from human observation, sat the primordial bisexual god Ometeotl, usually depicted as a male (Ometecuhtli) and female (Omecihuatl) pair. They were the ultimate creators of all other gods and humans; from their lofty perch in Omeyocan, the highest heaven, they sent to earth the souls of infants to be born. Remote as they were, they were also continuously active in the people's lives.

Below the earth's surface stretched the eight layers of the dark underworld, Mictlan.[6] Most people who died 'ordinary' deaths, whether king or commoner, young or old, male or female, were destined to spend their afterlives there. Their bodies were usually cremated, and their souls were sent on a harrowing journey through these layers, each of which presented a unique and often painful challenge such as a dangerous water passage, obsidian-bladed winds, being shot with arrows, and a place where their heart was eaten. After four perilous years, the soul finally arrived at the deepest region, the realm of Mictlantecuhtli and Mictlancihuatl, Lord and Lady of the Underworld. Fortunate souls would be aided in this journey by funerary offerings from their living relatives: a dog was a helpful guide and clothing, food, tobacco, *pulque*, jade beads and cacao were believed to ease the soul's trials.[7] It is worth noting that an individual who failed to live the 'exemplary life' might not receive these aids – an incentive to follow life's proper path.

Other afterlives were available to some Aztecs, those who died extraordinary deaths. Men who died in battle or as sacrifices followed the sun from its rising in the east to the zenith; women who died in childbirth carried the sun from the zenith to its setting in the west, where they hopped off at sunset and terrorized people foolish enough to wander out of their homes at night. These glorious afterlives rewarded the sacrifices made by these valiant individuals. Persons who died by drowning or other water-related causes were awarded an afterlife in Tlalocan, a pleasant, verdant paradise.

Tlalticpac (On the surface of the earth) was the horizontal terrestrial layer that tied together the celestial and underworld realms. Metaphorically, the earth's surface was visualized as a huge spiny alligator (*cipactli*) or an enormous toad-like earth monster (Tlaltecuhtli) that floated atop a primeval sea circling the landmass. The lands had been redeemed from the chaos of the fourth world destruction by divine sons of the creator deity, along with Quetzalcoatl and Tezcatlipoca, who hoisted the sky from the earth, holding it there as gigantic trees. The earth monster, having been mistreated by some of the gods, received pity from others who declared that thenceforth she would sustain the earth: her shoulders formed the mountains; her nose formed valleys; from her mouth emitted caves and rivers; from her hair grew trees and flowers; her skin supported grass and small plants; and her eyes provided springs, wells and small caves. It was the earth personified. And it was alive. These beliefs gave supernatural validation to what they saw around them on a daily basis. In the real world, they saw their lands surrounded by seas (at least to the east and west) and punctuated by meaningful landforms featured in the telling of their dramatic myths.

The landscape inhabited by the Aztecs was not only rich in natural resources. It was sacred. Natural features such as mountains, valleys, lakes, rivers, springs, whirlpools and caves were especially tied up in Aztec beliefs and targeted for serious ritual activities, from humble offerings to arduous pilgrimages. Mountains were especially revered, as they were associated with rainfall, crop fertility and curing. In one extraordinary ceremony, the three Triple Alliance rulers led an annual pilgrimage to a shrine on the summit of Mount Tlaloc, on the eastern edge of the Basin of Mexico. There, towards the end of the dry season in April or May, they made solemn offerings to petition the god Tlaloc for rain. Meanwhile, in Tenochtitlan worshippers erected an arbor on Tlaloc's side of the Great Temple, and along with a girl as a goddess impersonator, rowed the assemblage into Lake Texcoco to the mysterious whirlpool of Pantitlan. There, one of the trees was offered as a 'tree of life' and the girl was sacrificed.[8] Other natural features were revered for their special qualities: for instance, caves were viewed as entrances to the underworld, and Lake Texcoco was called Tonanhueyatl, or 'Great (or old) mother water'.

Human-made features on the landscape such as archaeological ruins and the Aztecs' own lofty temples also enjoyed sacred status. As already seen, the Classic site of Teotihuacan and Early Postclassic site of Tula both had potent sacred associations – the first with the creation of the fifth world, the latter with the shame of Quetzalcoatl. In their own age, the Mexica built their Great Temple at the very centre of their sacred world. To them, it was a human-made mountain, the Coatepec of mythic fame, whose summit served as a stage for epic re-enactments.

Gods and Goddesses

A number of gods and goddesses have already been mentioned in connection with myths and the structure of the universe, among them Huitzilopochtli, Coyolxauhqui, Quetzalcoatl, Tezcatlipoca and Tlaltecuhtli. These were but a few (albeit very important) deities in the vast Aztec pantheon, some of which were adopted from conquered city-states. Taken as a whole, the assemblage of these many deities and their overlapping and sometimes changeable attributes and insignia may seem at times bewildering to the Western mindset. Perhaps to complicate things even more, the general term for deity, *teotl*, could be attached to names of objects, acts and people (for instance, *teocuitlatl* was 'divine excrement' or gold, *teotlatolli* was 'divine speech', and *teochichimeca* referred to 'true Chichimecas'). Qualities of divinity extended to more than just gods and goddesses, although deities were especially divine.

True to the protean nature of Aztec divinity, Aztec deities often appear in different guises, depending on their role at the moment. Thus Quetzalcoatl was the wind (Ehecatl) before the onset of the rains, or Venus (Tlahuizcalpantecuhtli) at dawn, and could transform into an opossum or a monkey (in addition to his attributes already mentioned). Tezcatlipoca, as a magician and all-seeing wizard, became the god Mixcoatl to provide fire for humans, and also oversaw young warriors and was a culture anti-hero. Both Quetzalcoatl and Tezcatlipoca appear in hero tales. There were several goddesses that functioned as mother and earth deities, their names, roles and identifiers overlapping. The list goes on and on. Some of these variations were regional, but others were due to the dynamic nature of the cosmos where deities multitasked and altered their identities to adjust to changing situations. One must be flexible when deciphering the godly world of the Aztecs.

Despite these perplexities, the Aztec pantheon can be understood in terms of a limited number of Aztec concerns: celestial creativity, rain and agricultural fertility, and solar energy and warfare. The creator deities were omnipotent and often celebrated in colourful myths. At the highest heavenly layer, Ometeotl was distant and seems to have impinged only peripherally on the daily lives of the people. Tezcatlipoca (Smoking Mirror) was omnipotent but capricious: he could offer riches or inflict miseries, apparently on a whim. He was widely feared, since with his mirrors he could see everything in the universe. The god Xiuhtecuhtli presided over fire and every home's indispensable hearth. The other two primary themes, rain/fertility and solar energy/warfare, were daily life concerns. Their prominence in Aztec religion is highlighted by two of their major representatives, Tlaloc and Huitzilopochtli, sharing twin sanctuaries atop Tenochtitlan's Great Temple.

Fertility-related gods and goddesses commanded the greatest attention from Aztec worshippers: their very sustenance depended on the good will of deities presiding over rain, maize and the earth itself. Their interest in propitiating these deities was heightened during the frequent years of drought, floods and famine, and simply the historical knowledge of these catastrophes and the likelihood of their recurrence. Primary among these deities was Tlaloc, god of rain, who could be good (providing measured rains) or bad (deluging the landscape with floods). His female consort Chalchiuhtlicue (Jade-her-skirt) held sway over fresh waters. The earth itself was the domain of numerous mother goddesses: in addition to assuring the earth's fertility, they presided over matters such as pregnancy and birth, curing, and pleasure and feasting. Other deities in this cluster oversaw springtime, maize, maguey and *pulque*, games and gambling, and song and dance.

Solar energy and warfare also placed serious spiritual and ritual demands on every Aztec person. Deities in this cluster represented themes of the sun, death and the underworld, warfare and sacrifice, and notably included the powerful deities Tonatiuh (sun god), Mictlantecuhtli and Mictlancihuatl (Lord and Lady of the Underworld), and the Mexica patron god Huitzilopochtli. These deities were responsible for keeping the universe in motion and maintaining balance and harmony in that universe. On a practical level, the sun must rise daily, and the empire's military forces needed divine support in their endless wars.

Human sacrifice was integral to all of these themes. Myths and ceremonies constantly reinforced the belief that humans were burdened with a debt to their gods for their very existence. They must pay this never-ending debt with their blood and sometimes with their lives, most frequently having their hearts removed.[9] Some individuals were reverently sacrificed as godly impersonators, others were stretched on the sacrificial block as war captives. In either case, it was always a ritual event, even though late in the empire massive sacrifices also served to proclaim and boost a ruler's power. On a more philosophical plane, the Aztecs believed that life and death were deeply entwined: sacrifice to a solar deity energized the Sun's daily movements, and human blood was understood to nourish the ever-needy earth.

Many deities were honoured as patrons of ethnic, occupational or territorial groups. For instance, Toci was patroness of midwives and curers, Xochiquetzal oversaw weavers and embroiderers, Xochipilli was patron of painters, Yacatecuhtli travelled with intrepid merchants, and the goldsmiths looked to Xipe Totec. City-states and *calpolli* enjoyed their own patrons: Huitzilopochtli was patron of the Mexica of Tenochtitlan, Tezcatlipoca of Texcoco, Camaxtli of Tlaxcalla, Quetzalcoatl of Cholula and so on. To properly worship them, every god and goddess had their own temples where they were physically represented as mostly anthropomorphic

A human sacrifice. A priest ritually removes a heart at the top of a temple's steps.

statues in stone, wood, clay, rubber or copal resin, and even as images made of amaranth seeds. Each temple had its own dedicated priests and sometimes priestesses. Considering the great number of deities, and that these deities were worshipped in communities throughout the realm, there must have been many thousands of persons engaged as religious officials and servants. These individuals not only served their deities and maintained their temples, but supervised required periodic ceremonies.

Ceremonies

The world of the supernatural was brought down to earth through the performance of a great many ceremonies, private and public. Private ceremonies were household-based, and the typical household maintained a shrine or altar at which rituals were conducted daily. Other ceremonies were primarily focused on momentous life-cycle transitions, especially birth and naming, marriage and death. These events consisted of prescribed activities. A wedding, for instance, required the services of matchmakers and astrologers, and input from relatives near and far. Arranging a marriage was time-consuming, with a great deal of consulting, gift-giving, feasting, drinking, dancing and endless lectures by elders reinforcing principles of exemplary behaviour. It was a costly affair for any family, with foods, cacao, flowers and tobacco ideally available, although the lavishness of the event depended on the economic wherewithal of the families. Similar economic investments were made for births and funerals, as families and neighbours welcomed new members or sent them to their afterlives. Other rituals were celebrated by specialized groups on designated days in honour of their patron deity: for instance, merchants felt free to display their considerable wealth on Four Wind, rulers bestowed gifts on their palace workers on One Flower, and slaves were granted special treatment by Tezcatlipoca on the day One Death. On any day, somewhere in the realm, it could be assumed that someone was celebrating something.

Public ceremonies were performed on the grand stages of every city-state. Some gala events celebrated special events such as a temple dedication, troops returning from the battlefield, tribute deliveries from distant lands, a king's coronation or a king's funeral. But the most anticipated and predictable ceremonies were those that revolved around the eighteen solar months, and were enacted at the beginning or end of each of these twenty-day periods. Each ceremony was tailored to the demands of the month's presiding deity and was characterized by its unique purpose and agenda, sequence of events, cast of participants and ritual paraphernalia. Each month was celebrated with elaborate household and public ceremonies, some of them punctuated with flamboyant displays and dramatic human sacrifices. Most of the ceremonies required participation by a wide spectrum of the population: priests were always front and centre, but also rulers danced, nobles feasted, women and girls leaped about, youths and maidens fought mock battles, children were ritually 'stretched' to make them grow tall, elders sang ancient songs, farmer families offered the fruits of their labours and artisans honoured their patron deities. Communal participation was essential to the proper performance of the ceremonies and, hence, their efficacy.

The monthly ceremonies typically began with fasting or feasting and ended with feasting. In between were scripted processions, singing and dancing to music,[10] offerings and animal and/or human sacrifices. For example, Tlaxochimaco (Offering of Flowers), the ninth month of the year, was celebrated in the middle of the summer (the rainy season). The honoured god of the month was Huitzilopochtli and the rituals were lively and colourful. Before the big event beautiful flowers were collected and strung into garlands, and great quantities of tamales were made. After a sleepless night (from anticipation), participants adorned Huitzilopochtli and other gods with the flower garlands; this was followed by household feasting and a great deal of singing and graceful dancing, apparently in public venues. At the end of the day, in their homes everyone sang reverent songs to their special deities and elderly men and women enjoyed copious quantities of *pulque*. During the long celebration, people from all rungs of the social ladder wended their way from their homes to the capital city's main temple, then back again, performing scripted components of the overall ceremony at home and in public.

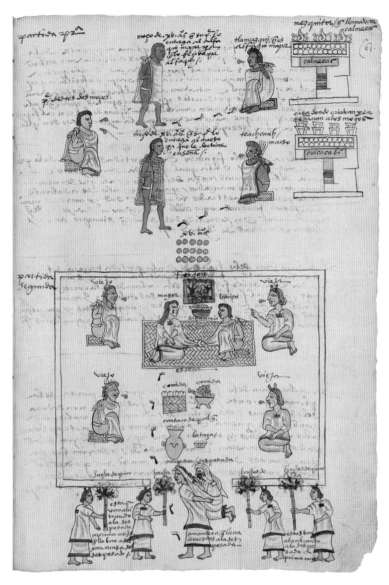

A wedding ceremony, literally tying the knot.

Offerings were central to all Aztec ceremonies, and reinforced the theme of reciprocity that was essential to human–deity relations. Deities expected offerings from humans, and humans expected some favour (from rain to a battlefield victory) in return.[11] Offerings served to integrate households into these public ceremonies, as individuals spent days at home cooking tamales, stringing flowers or making offerings at their domestic shrines, all in connection with the grand ceremony. Food, flowers and incense were common offerings, but sacrifices of live animals (usually quail) and humans punctuated the events of several of the ceremonies. Other offerings, apparently commemorating special events such as temple expansions, were densely packed throughout the sacred precinct surrounding Tenochtitlan's Great Temple. More than two hundred of these buried offerings have been uncovered to date (with excavations ongoing). These offerings contain tens of thousands of artefacts, ranging from precious stones and metals to ceramics, obsidian and relics from earlier cultures. Dominant among the offerings were animals: more than 450 species from the full range of imperial environments have been identified in the sacred precinct caches. Human skeletal remains of sacrificed warriors, children and high-ranking individuals have also been uncovered in this urban ceremonial centre.[12]

In Tenochtitlan, eleven of the flamboyant eighteen monthly ceremonies were dedicated to Tlaloc and his fertility associates, suggesting a concern or even apprehension about rain and fertility. The remaining months focused on celestial creation and warfare, with Huitzilopochtli or Tezcatlipoca taking precedence (see Table of Monthly Ceremonies). Additional ceremonies took place at longer intervals: those devoted to the fire god every four years, rituals requiring extensive fasting appearing every eight years, and the especially stressful ceremonies enacted at the end of every 52-year calendrical cycle. Worried about the imminent ending of the world, people smashed their household possessions and extinguished their fires as priests led a solemn precession to a nearby hill. There, a man was sacrificed by heart extraction and a 'new' fire was ignited in his chest. That fire was passed from person to person and from community to community until the entire land was renewed for an additional 52 years. A great collective sigh of relief must have swept across the land.

What did all these extraordinary events mean to the individual? Repeated exposure to and participation in theatrical public ceremonies reiterated the culture's mythical underpinnings and reaffirmed the Aztecs' belief in the interplay between life and death through human sacrifices. Domestic rituals reinforced ethics and codes of conduct at key moments in people's lives. Overall, whether on private or public stages, ceremonies were occasions for reciprocal interactions and were designed to establish (and re-establish) balance and harmony among all players in the human, natural and supernatural worlds. The world was viewed as uncertain, disorderly and potentially catastrophic. Serious periodic Aztec ceremonies brought order, equilibrium and hopefully divine favour to this chaotic cosmos.

All of this was upended with the Spanish arrival. Or was it?

TEN

THE END OF THE FIFTH AGE: THE SETTING SUN

You said that our gods are not true gods. New words are these that you speak; because of them we are disturbed, because of them we are troubled. For our ancestors before us, who lived upon the earth, were unaccustomed to speak thus. From them have we inherited our pattern of life which in truth they did hold; in reverence they held, they honored, our gods. They taught us all their rules of worship, all their ways of honoring the gods. Thus before them, do we prostrate ourselves; in their names we bleed ourselves; our oaths we keep, incense we burn, and sacrifices we offer . . . And now, are we to destroy the ancient order of life? . . . Hear, oh Lords, do nothing to our people that will bring misfortune upon them, that will cause them to perish . . . We cannot be tranquil, and yet we certainly do not believe; we do not accept your teachings as truth, even though this may offend you.[1]

Using these measured but unyielding words, Aztec *tlamatinime* (wise men)[2] confronted twelve newly arrived Franciscan friars in colonial Mexico in 1524. The setting was the Spaniards' new urban hub, Mexico City, being constructed directly atop the Aztecs' Tenochtitlan, now three years after that city's fall. The job of the friars was to convert the 'heathens' to Christianity, and in the broader exchange they presented their case for the primacy of their god and the falsity of the native pantheon.

The purpose of the *tlamatinime* statement, some of it quoted above, was to courteously welcome the friars but to unwaveringly convey their loyalty to their own traditional gods. Recognizing their subservience to the new lords of the land, they nonetheless reiterated the centrality of their own deities in the creation of all things, and their staunch obligations to continue to serve their ancestors and their own gods with their traditional rituals. Game on.

By the mid-sixteenth century dramatic (and often traumatic) changes had occurred and adjustments had been made to the new situation by both native people and Spaniards. Compromises were frequent and functional. As a case in point, the featherwork mosaic triptych seen here represents the blending of indigenous technology and craftsmanship with Spanish Christian formats and symbolism. Triptychs were unknown in ancient Mexico, but these altar cards were common religious objects in the Christian world. Therefore, the structure of this object in three attached segments (made of wood with a giltwood frame) may have been created by Spanish artisans, although Spanish observers often commented on the facility with which native artisans learned new techniques.

Unquestionably, the creation of the feather mosaics was an indigenous effort. Close examination of the piece reveals coloured paper and several colours of feathers: pink, yellow, orange, white, brown, blue, green and black.[3] Green and blue hummingbird feathers are scattered throughout: broad areas that today appear grey were most likely covered with these iridescent hummingbird feathers in the sixteenth century. This 'feather painting' must have been radiant and stunning, competing for attention with its church's stained-glass windows. The lettering and other fine lines may have been formed with great-tailed grackle feathers. The artisans were so skilled and meticulous that they could fashion the small objects on the table, the graceful folds of clothing, layers of bricks, legible lettering and even the saints' toes, all from carefully sliced feathers. The result is a feather mosaic drawing based on ancient technologies, but applying those skills to a new format, style and set of symbols.

The symbolism is Christian: the central panel features the Crucifixion and the Last Supper above a Latin text that reads 'For

A mid-16th-century feather mosaic triptych with Christian motifs.

this is my body. For this is the chalice of my blood of the new and eternal testament, the mystery of the faith which shall be shed for you and for many for the remission of sins.' The left panel illustrates St Peter holding the keys of heaven and the right shows St Paul with a sword. The composition as a whole is interesting in that the three panels appear to have been executed by three different feather-workers: a master artisan creating the detailed and complex central piece and two somewhat less proficient artisans producing the side panels.[4] The featherworker fashioning the left panel appears to be more accomplished than his colleague on the right, although they produced symmetrical imagery with their saints and backgrounds. This suggests a coordinated team effort, following indigenous pat-terns of production carried over from pre-Hispanic times. So we have here a Spanish-style object made with native featherworking techniques applied to Christian motifs and symbolism. Here, the two cultures have met and compromised, resulting in an extraor-dinarily affective religious object.[5] It encapsulates the meeting and meshing of two worlds, which took place on cultural, economic, social, political and religious planes. How did all of this unfold, from the native point of view?

Chapter One of this book offers a glimpse of the conquest of the Aztecs through Spanish eyes. The rest of this chapter looks at these momentous events and their consequences from the vantage point of the indigenous inhabitants.

A Capsule of Events, February 1519–August 1521

In February 1519 Hernando Cortés sailed from Cuba with eleven ships, sixteen horses and about six hundred men, of whom between fifty and one hundred were sailors. He was headed for the Mexican mainland. His voyage had been preceded by two others that had skirted the coast of Yucatán and skirmished with some of the natives, one in 1517 headed by Hernandez de Córdoba and another in 1518 led by Juan de Grijalva. These forays were important in providing Cortés with at least 38 seasoned men for his company. Neither of the 1517 or 1518 expeditions forged far inland. Cortés's campaign did.

Cortés first sailed along the coast of Yucatán where he picked up the invaluable Jerónimo de Aguilar, who had been marooned there since 1511 and had become conversant in the Yucatec Mayan language. After a violent encounter with the natives in Tabasco, Cortés was presented with valuable gifts, including twenty native women. One of these was Malinche (later baptized Marina), who was bilingual in Nahuatl and Chontal Mayan and was to become Cortés's translator and companion, bearing him a child, Martín.

Landing near present-day Veracruz city, Cortés and his company established a town and moved inland, first to Cempoalla and then to Tlaxcalla. Both were large indigenous polities that ultimately allied with the Spaniards. Cempoalla was subject to the Aztec empire but resented paying tributes, and Tlaxcalla had always been independent from that powerful empire. The Mexica king was well informed of the Spaniards' arrival and march from the coast, at first sending messengers with gifts and then, growing apprehensive, attempting to block their route with maguey plants. A story emerged in later years that the Mexica thought the Spaniards were gods, but there is little contemporary foundation for this. In Camilla Townsend's words, 'The Mexica did not believe in people becoming gods, or in gods coming to earth only in one particular year, or in anybody having a preordained right to conquer them.'[6]

On 8 November 1519 Motecuhzoma came to the edge of Tenochtitlan to meet Cortés. The Spaniards and many of their Tlaxcallan allies were allowed to enter the city and were housed in downtown Tenochtitlan in the expansive palace of Motecuhzoma's father, Axayacatl. Uneasy relations continued in Tenochtitlan until mid-summer 1520. Initially interactions were tentatively amiable and the Spaniards were treated as honoured guests (even enjoying a tour of the city), but then Cortés assaulted the image of the god Huitzilopochtli (which won him no favour with the priests) and took the Mexica king hostage, placing him in irons. More Spaniards arrived from Cuba to bring Cortés back to the island, but Cortés met these Spaniards on the coast and convinced them to join him. In his absence, his second-in-command, the impetuous Pedro de Alvarado, had attacked and killed many Mexica while they were celebrating their monthly ceremony of Toxcatl. When Cortés returned to Tenochtitlan he found his men and allies under attack in Axayacatl's palace. At this point Cortés had about 1,000 men, nearly one hundred horses and about 2,000 Tlaxcallans with him. The Spanish position in the city soon became untenable, especially after the death of Motecuhzoma.[7] On a drizzly July night the Spaniards stealthily retreated from the city via the Tlacopan causeway. The fighting was fierce and the Spaniards and their Tlaxcallan allies suffered disastrous losses – perhaps as many as six hundred Spanish and most of the Tlaxcallan lives were lost, along with many horses. The Spaniards called that night the *Noche Triste*, or 'Sad Night'. For the Mexica it was not so sad; to them it was 'the night the Spaniards died at the Tolteca Canal'.

Harassed by the Mexica for some distance, the Spaniards retreated to Tlaxcalla where they received a lukewarm welcome (the Tlaxcallans had lost many men in this expedition). Nonetheless, for the next five and a half months they were hosted by the Tlaxcallans and healed, regrouped, assembled ship parts and convinced many other native city-states to join them. In late December the Spaniards and their allies marched on the island city. In the meantime, in Tenochtitlan the Mexica had crowned their new ruler, Motecuhzoma's brother Cuitlahuac, who died a few months later of smallpox. He was replaced by Cuauhtemoc, Motecuhzoma's cousin. Anticipating another attack, the Mexica walled up roads, obstructed canals and urban passageways, planted pointed stakes in the lake, and tried to assure the loyalty of their nearby allies (with small success). By the time the Spaniards laid siege to the island city, a great many surrounding lakeshore city-states had sided with them and Tenochtitlan was now almost isolated. On 28 April 1521 the Spaniards formally laid siege to the great city of Tenochtitlan, whose people were already weakened by famine and Spanish-introduced disease. Cortés now commanded over nine hundred Spaniards (more had arrived from Cuba), many thousands of native allies, 86 horses, fifteen cannons and thirteen brigantines. After 75 days of intense fighting, the city finally fell with the capture of its king Cuauhtemoc on 13 August 1520.[8] Although Tenochtitlan had fallen, it took concerted military expeditions over the next several decades to subdue many of the other peoples in Mesoamerica.

Entire districts of the city were largely demolished and sacked, and the population devastated. Casualties are extremely difficult to estimate and range from 100,000 to 240,000 Mexica fatalities. Spanish losses may have reached one hundred dead during the siege (about half of them captured and sacrificed).[9] Losses by the native allies are virtually impossible to estimate, although one estimate places 24,000 indigenous allies at the siege of Tenochtitlan.[10] It was those native allies, with their own agendas, who provided the Spaniards with the large fighting force in this conflict. Although Spanish weaponry is often mentioned as pre-eminent in the conquest,[11] it was largely the native peoples themselves, waging war as they had for centuries (or even millennia), that secured the outcome.

The Native View of the Conquest

The Aztecs lived in the Fifth World, or Fifth Sun, destined to be destroyed by earthquakes. Little did they know that instead their destruction would come at the hands of strangers from across the eastern sea: Spaniards seeking gold, souls and elevated status. Tenochtitlan fell to these invaders on the day Ome Xocotl uetzi Ce Coatl (13 August 1521 in the Christian calendar) with the capture of the Mexica king Cuauhtemoc. His name, translated as Descending Eagle or Setting Sun, is sadly appropriate.

Native accounts of the conquest offer insights into how the Aztecs assimilated the new and unknown into their known world, how they understood and misunderstood their enemy, and who took credit for the victory. They reveal details into Aztec motivations, priorities, choices and actions. A few pithy examples illustrate these themes and address some of the more mystifying enigmas of the events of those years.

Fitting the new into the old

The native Chalcan writer Chimalpahin viewed the Spaniards as another ethnic group not terribly unlike the many such entities that populated the Aztec domain.[12] This notion fitted well into their world view and meant that they confronted the Spaniards in familiar ways, at least for a time. So they met the Spaniards and courteously talked with them, tried to convince the Spaniards of their superiority, and met them head-on on the battlefield – all well-worn indigenous tactics. They did not immediately take into account that their adversary played by different rules and had different motivations and priorities. For instance, on the battlefield, native fighters were willing to take serious bodily risks in attempts to capture their enemies for later sacrifice; the Spaniards had no such goal and did not hesitate to cut down their fierce foes at close quarters. Nonetheless, some Spaniards were captured, as were some horses, and both men and horses were dealt with as were their traditional enemies: sacrifice and decapitation followed by the stringing of the heads on prominent skull racks. In the meantime, Aztec warriors did not hesitate to take up Spanish weaponry when available, wielding swords with apparent dexterity. There is one particularly enigmatic matter: allowing the Spaniards into the confines of Tenochtitlan was one thing, but allowing the Tlaxcallans into the city was quite another. Why did the Mexica do this? Here history comes to our rescue, as the same Motecuhzoma

A native warrior wields a Spanish sword.

who ruled in 1519 had also, some years earlier, allowed their arch-enemies the Huexotzinca into Tenochtitlan as refugees from their other arch-enemies, the Tlaxcallans. So the entry of traditional enemies into the confines of their powerful city was not completely new to the Mexica. In any event, it is possible that the Tlaxcallans that did accompany Cortés into the city were unarmed porters, not armed warriors, and therefore not considered a threat by the Mexica.

Understanding and misunderstanding the enemy

The first great obstacle in cross-cultural encounters is understanding each other's language. Cortés was lucky: he had with him Aguilar, who spoke Spanish and Yucatec Mayan, and Marina, who spoke Chontal Mayan and Nahuatl. An encounter with a Nahua lord might look like this: the Nahua lord spoke in Nahuatl to

Marina, she translated from Nahuatl and spoke in Chontal Mayan to Aguilar, who understood the Mayan and translated the message into Spanish for Córtes, who then spoke, and the somewhat cumbersome scenario was played in reverse. It apparently worked well enough, although it is not known how much was lost in these translations. There were signs of misunderstandings. There was the matter of the momentous meeting between Motecuhzoma and Cortés: the Aztec ruler was welcoming and performing proper etiquette in his speech (being an 'exemplary person'); Cortés interpreted Motecuhzoma's speech as a surrender and crafted a good story to relate this to the Spanish king. As another example, when the Spaniards demanded gold, and the natives provided it, the natives hoped their generous gifts would satisfy the newcomers' needs. But they underestimated the Spanish greed for gold and their gifts only whetted their appetite for more. There would never be enough gold.

Who won the war?

It was important to the conquistadores that they portray themselves as victors against overwhelming odds. Yes, the Spaniards were repeatedly outnumbered by their native foes, but they were also outnumbered by their own native allies. Chief among these were the Tlaxcallans, who judged that 'with Spanish assistance they would be able to destroy the Mexica army and its capital city.'[13] By this thinking, the Spaniards were not the primary victors, the Tlaxcallans were. Similarly, with different battle lines drawn, the Huexotzinca, often allied with Tlaxcalla against the Aztec empire but with their own interests at the forefront, 'sought to use the Spanish presence to promote their interests and pursue rivalries first against the Mexica and later against the Tlaxcalans.'[14] The Spaniards were seeking a victory by exploiting long-standing animosities among native groups; the native groups were using the Spaniards to promote their primacy in conflicts among themselves. They undoubtedly envisioned a realignment of the native political environment with the help of the newcomers. In these conflicting perceptions, the only losers would be the Mexica and those who stood with them at the end. Regardless of who anticipated victory, ultimately the Spaniards unseated the traditional dynasties of all of New Spain's city-states.[15]

We are afforded additional glimpses into the events of the conflict from the native perspective and their sources of information. For instance, when the Spaniards arrived at Chalco, two of the local kings went out to meet Cortés, another ran to Tenochtitlan to join ranks with Motecuhzoma, and another fled into hiding with all of his wives. Similar schisms occurred in Texcoco and Tenochtitlan, and surely in other undocumented polities. Native responses to the Spanish arrival were not necessarily uniform, and factions often broke unevenly along kinship, residential or ethnic lines. Also native accounts reveal the apprehension the Mexica felt as they awaited the arrival of the Spaniards, their fear of the ferocious dogs and their amazement at the Spaniards' obsession with bright shiny things. We hear about their efficient messenger systems, how they mourned and disposed of their dead, and how they prepared for ceremonies and for war. We also learn about the feats of their own warrior-heroes, how they threw a captured cannon into the lake, how they quickly adjusted to Spanish firepower by ducking and weaving, and the effectiveness of native canoes alongside Spanish brigantines during the siege. We also can listen to speeches and dialogues, learn a great deal about individuals' names and titles, and visualize details of the local geography.

The People

Motecuhzoma's successor, Cuitlahuac, died of smallpox even before the siege of Tenochtitlan began. He was not alone. The native people suddenly encountered unfamiliar diseases, including smallpox, measles, influenza and possibly typhus, to which they had no resistance. After the conquest they died in unprecedented numbers in calamitous epidemics that hit in 1545–7, 1576–81 and 1629–31. In the Basin of Mexico, estimates of population loss range from one-half to five-sixths within half a century after the conquest. Losses were uneven. Otompan lost a full half of its people in the 1576–81 epidemic. By 1563 Xochimilco's numbers reportedly dropped from 30,000 to 7,000–8,000.[16] By the end of the sixteenth century the native population of the Morelos region (just south of the Basin of Mexico) declined by 75–80 per cent, and some lowland communities were lost entirely. At the beginning of the seventeenth century estimates place the native population of central Mexico at just over 1 million, down from 12–15 million in 1519. Overall, it is usually estimated that the native population of the Americas as a whole suffered a 90 per cent loss within a hundred years or so of contact.

The consequences of these losses were traumatic and far-reaching. Famine was widespread. Some community crafts and specialized knowledge were lost as their participants disappeared. And with so many communities thinned out, Spanish clerics were encouraged to concentrate the natives in larger communities for conversion purposes, uprooting survivors from their traditional lands and lives.

The arrival and establishment of Spaniards in what was now called New Spain affected the native people in other ways. Mostly men early on, Spaniards married native women who bore *mestizo* (mied blood, mixed heritage) children. Adding to the increasingly complicated population mix were Africans who arrived primarily as slaves. Since most Spanish settlements coincided with areas of large native settlements, 'the black slaves of Spaniards in the colonies tended to function more as personal auxiliaries – as domestic servants, as assistants in commercial enterprises, as symbols of social status – just as in the Conquest they were personal auxiliaries of individual Spanish conquistadors.'[17] Perhaps dozens of these armed servants were freed and became conquistadors in their own right. Later conquest expeditions engaged many more Africans, and in 1537 reportedly 10,000 Africans resided in Mexico City.[18]

Expectedly, the arrival of new lords of the land disrupted the native social hierarchy. Commoners' lives became realigned: they now became subservient to Spanish overlords, much as they had served their native rulers and lords in pre-Spanish times. Colonialism also had its impact on the hereditary kings and nobles: those who cooperated were rewarded by the Spaniards; those who resisted were punished and lost their offices (and sometimes their lives). While some of the indigenous elites held on to lands, tribute-paying commoners and high political offices, these rights became eroded over time until nobles and commoners became compressed into a single (low) social status under colonial rule. Following time-worn traditions, natives of all statuses continued to refer to themselves by their *altepetl* affiliations or, more generally, as *nican titlaca* (we people here), and later on, as *macehualtin* (commoners).

Spaniards in New Spain preferred living in urban centres and they typically built their towns and cities on the ruins of the native towns and cities. Mexico City was constructed on top of a largely razed Tenochtitlan, the worked stones of the pre-Spanish buildings used for new Spanish governmental, religious and domestic structures. About one hundred years after the conquest, Fernando de Alva Ixtlilxochitl (descendant of Texcocan royalty) mused that Texcoco's magnificent royal palace had become, by that time, a Spanish workshop.

Sometimes Spaniards founded new cities such as Puebla and the port city of Veracruz to foster their administrative, economic and religious agendas. Cities in colonial Mexico, and especially Mexico City, were the nucleii of Spanish government and life. Once the native people were conquered and their lands occupied, some newly arrived Spaniards were awarded *encomiendas* (grants of native communities and labour) and fanned out into broader regions. By the mid-sixteenth century Spaniards were residing in many indigenous towns that had native majorities; some of these towns (such as Tlaxcalla) maintained native councils, but the authority of these political entities became more and more diminished by the early seventeenth century.

Old and New Economies

Almost from the moment of contact, Aztecs and Spaniards were exposed to each other's foods, material goods and natural resources. The Spaniards ate native food, toured the Tlatelolco marketplace and searched for sources of gold. Conversely, the Aztecs and their neighbours encountered sailing ships and horses (which they called 'deer'), and faced steel weapons and armour. Each side became aware of even more novelties during the course of the sixteenth century.

Among the major Spanish introductions were European crops. Wheat, as the Spaniards' primary staple crop, came to occupy some tracts of land previously devoted to maize, although the indigenous people continued to prefer maize in their diets. Grapes also were planted, primarily for the production of wine (for secular and ceremonial drinking), and plantation crops such as sugarcane were introduced in lowland regions.

Introduced domesticated animals included cattle, horses, donkeys, mules, pigs, goats, sheep and chickens. In early colonial times the use of cattle, horses, mules and donkeys was generally restricted to Spaniards, native elites and merchants. Sheep and goat herding enjoyed broader popularity and these animals were owned by native entrepreneurs and even entire communities. For instance, Tlaxcalla's town council owned a herd of sheep in the mid-1500s, though lacking experience in this enterprise they hired a Spaniard to manage the herds. Nonetheless, livestock ownership in general was in Spanish hands during the sixteenth century and caused problems to native cultivators: large tracts of agricultural land were converted to pasturage, uncontained animals at times destroyed nearby crops, humans and animals sometimes competed for the same food supply, and, on an individual level, one native complained in court of being trampled by a horse. But it was the less expensive chicken, resembling the native turkey and easily raised around a house, that readily took hold in native communities.

Other introductions included metal tools that arrived in the form of machetes, knives, ploughs, hoes and scissors, and the use of the wheel for transport, spinning threads and throwing pots. Maguey plants continued to provide popular drinks, but now in addition to the fermented *pulque*, people were producing distilled tequila. Native beeswax was now used in candle making. Guitars and other stringed instruments gained prominence in the native musical repertoire. Changes occurred in the production of textiles and clothing. Sheep yielded wool – today sheep are still called *ichcatl* (cotton) by Nahuatl-speakers. Heavy-duty treadle looms were introduced to weave the wool (and spinning wheels to spin it into threads); these were operated by men in cramped workshops. However, women continued to hand spin threads and weave clothing (adding wool to their materials) on backstrap looms in their homes. Indeed, the persistence of indigenous clothing, diet, crafts and agricultural practices was remarkable. In many cases there was a merging of the traditional and the introduced. Take the case of clothing. Native clothing was essentially draped; the Spaniards introduced tailored clothing such as blouses, shirts and breeches. Women continued to wear their traditional skirts, now topped by a Spanish-style blouse that was furthermore sometimes topped by a native cape (*quechquemitl*). Men now tied their traditional capes over Spanish shirts and breeches. These styles, for men and women, have persisted to the present day and are known as 'Indian clothing', even though they are hybrids dating from colonial times.

These many introductions would change the ways the native people went about their daily lives, to greater or lesser degrees. In particular, some of these introductions reoriented land use

A 20th-century Nahua woman spins wool on her traditional spindle; a backstrap loom with wool sits beside her.

hazer vestidos conforme ala
proporcion del cuerpo, y echar
alamares y aireles, alfin
haze todo su poder, por dar
contento alos dueños delas
ropas.

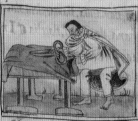

¶ El mal sastre, vsa engaño y
fraude enel officio, hurta loq́
puede, y lo que sobra del pa
ño, todo lo toma para si, y
cose mal, y da puntadas lar
gas, y pide mas deloque es jus
to por el trabajo. Ni sabe hazer
cortesia, sino que es muy tia
no

¶ El hilado detieso o de su

moiolnonotzani, tlacematini,
Hacemanani, Hatzoma, tlacaloa,
tlatencuepa, tlatemimiloa, ten
quatonoa, tlatepitzco, tlatepitzi
tzoma, melaoac, itech netlacane
co, tlapanitia, tepanitia, tepan
tia, tlatlamachotia, tlatlama
chia, tlaiecchioa, tlatlamachto
toquia, tlaquecimachtlalia, te
tech momictia, tetechmocencaoa
¶ Intlaueliloc tlatzonqui: teca
mocacaiaoani, teca mauiltiani,
ichtequini, tlanaoatl chioani, tla
ixpachoani, motlacauiani, tla
ciuhcachioani, tlapoxaoacahi
tzomani, tlapapaçoni, tlapapa
co tlacuecueço, tlaneneçuilço
tlapapaçoloa, tetetemachia, a
monenpololtani, tlamatataca
tematataca, amocotontlani,
idotequi, matzinalloti, tlainaia
¶ Tzauhqui: intzauhqui tlama

                              25

and labour. Natives attached to *encomiendas* needed to learn the particularities of growing new crops and raising unfamiliar animals. Plantation crops drew on slave labour from Africa. Spanish mining enterprises moved native labourers from their communities to distant mining sites. Even with these changes, native people could still rely on the traditional marketplace, *tianquiztli*, for their familiar material things and social interactions. But new commodities such as candles, shirts, wool capes, machetes and chicken eggs now appeared alongside their known goods. Some additional marketplace adjustments were made. The Aztec five-day market schedule was realigned to fit into the Spanish seven-day week, and Spanish monies (*pesos* and *tomines*) gained popularity, although cacao-bean money continued in use for many decades.

This process worked in both directions. Spain (and the rest of the world generally) received many products from Mexico and other parts of the Americas, including maize, potatoes, tomatoes, chillies, avocados, vanilla, turkeys, tobacco, cochineal dyes, rubber and, of course, the all-important chocolate. Some of these have become so entrenched in their new lands that it is now inconceivable to think of Italian food without tomatoes, or a world without Swiss or Belgian chocolates.

Old and New Religions

Along with Spanish conquistadores, administrators and settlers came regular and secular Christian clergy. They came from a world that had very recently (1492) seized the Iberian Peninsula from nearly eight centuries of Moorish control, and was currently in the throes of a religious inquisition. Arriving in New Spain, Spanish ecclesiastics encountered people worshipping many deities, adoring idols and engaging in human sacrifice. They faced a religion that readily assimilated deities and their paraphernalia from conquered regions. People's lives were ordered through performances of demanding rituals based on calendrical schedules. These theatrical ceremonies, sometimes re-enactments of dramatic myths, were punctuated with music, singing, dancing, processions, fasting, feasting, offerings and often human sacrifice. While these were periodic, every day people were reminded of their religious obligations: visually, temples were the tallest and most centrally located structures in any community. How much of this changed under colonial Spanish rule? The Christian clergy was bent on large-scale religious conversion. How did that work out in the decades following the conquest?

Early on, temples were demolished and churches were built atop their foundations or nearby: the Spaniards appropriated locations charged with potent spiritual meaning. Christian icons replaced native idols. The native priests had no place in the new religious system and essentially lost their jobs, although individuals who may have been trained as priests in the Aztec world found niches in the colonial world as scribes or other professionals, especially serving Spanish friars or priests. A new calendar was imposed, Christian festivals and processions replaced Aztec ones, and Christian-themed plays became popular entertainments that reinforced Christian stories and principles (but also included native subtleties of expression and meaning).

Still, in this dynamic setting many native religious beliefs and practices persisted. For instance, native specialists such as midwives and curers continued to provide personal or household services. And while the friars and priests often claimed triumphant inroads into religious conversion, by the mid-sixteenth century it had become clear that conversion was accommodation at best. Yes, Dios had been generally accepted, but this was standard practice among the Aztecs who were accustomed to adopting other people's gods and adding them to their own repertoire. It did not mean their other gods had been forsaken, as the Spaniards had hoped. Under pressure of conversion but determined to retain their traditional beliefs, native people coupled their gods with the newly arrived potpourri of saints. These meshings were not random: for example, the Virgin Mary and the Aztec mother goddess Tonantzin merged into the Virgin of Guadalupe, Jesus Christ became associated with Tonatiuh (the sun), John the Baptist (associated with water) was coupled with Tlaloc (the rain god) and St Anne (Jesus's grandmother) was linked to Toci (Our Grandmother).

These meshings seem fairly straightforward and even predictable, but other matters were more nuanced and full of
misunderstandings. For instance, the Spanish clergy, trying to
emphasize the concept of good versus evil, cast it in terms of the
Aztec concept of order and chaos. But these were not parallel concepts, as the Aztec duality was not an opposition: rather order and
chaos complemented one another, much as did light and darkness,
and life and death. A subtle near-miss. Another example involves
the concept of hell: the Aztecs believed in an underworld as a
destination after death, but it did not carry the values associated
with the Christian hell – it was not a region of punishment. The
clergy were convinced they had successfully conveyed their concept as their flock indicated that they understood that place well.
But their flock was thinking of something quite different. By the
end of the sixteenth century, conversion to Christianity was
uneven at best.[19]

The triptych at the beginning of this chapter is a good example
of the complexities of religious syncretism in sixteenth-century
Mexico. The figures and symbols decorating the object represent
an entirely new religion brought into the artisans' land by the new
Spanish overlords. On this one object the craftsmen deftly applied
their well-honed traditional skills to novel images; it serves as a
microcosm of the innumerable ways in which the indigenous
people coped with and adapted to their new and often traumatic
circumstances.

ELEVEN

THE AZTEC LEGACY: REALITY AND IMAGINATION

These are my *nahualli*.[1]

It was the last day of our 1985 field season. We had been researching traditional backstrap loom weaving practices among women in the Sierra Norte de Puebla, Mexico. I was interviewing a weaver about an intricate textile she had been weaving. She described the materials, techniques, time commitments, costs and other practical details. When I asked her about the designs, she said, 'These are my *nahualli*.' *Nahualli* are animal spirit companions and derive from ancient pre-Columbian times. I found myself marvelling at the animals as they stared at me from this newly woven textile; while ancient in origin, they were a meaningful part of the world of this twentieth-century woman and her neighbours. How pervasive was this belief among the people of this community? How and why did it survive the centuries? Did it mean the same thing to these people as it did to their ancestors? My mind was bombarded with question after question. Frustratingly, this was the last day of that field season, and the answers would have to wait. But the gist of this revelation was clear: this piece of culture, and many others, had persisted for nearly five centuries of culture contact and change, some of it highly traumatic. How do these continuities manifest themselves in our modern world?

Aztec Descendants

More than 2 million people speak the Nahuatl language today. The weaver who lent me profound insights into her culture is one of them. She lives in a small community in the Sierra Norte de Puebla, but Nahuatl-speakers (Nahua) live in at least fifteen states in Mexico – in villages, towns and cities – and in other countries to which they have migrated. Many of them, especially the younger generations, are bilingual with Spanish or other languages.

When asked what language she speaks, this woman and other people in the region respond 'Mexicano' (Me-shee-KA-no): Mexican, or 'language of the Mexica'. Of course, she lives far from the Mexica heartland and their gleaming city Tenochtitlan, in both time and space. Yet variations of the Nahuatl language were spoken in pockets throughout the Aztec imperial domain (including this region); the language use was further expanded after the 1521 conquest as Nahua warriors often accompanied Spanish forces of conquest beyond the Aztec heartland. This is not to say that the Nahuatl-speaking people of this region, distant from the Basin of Mexico, were direct descendants of the Mexica – probably not. But they nonetheless share a constellation of pan-Mesoamerican (and more specifically Nahua) cultural attributes, even across long distances and through nearly five hundred years.[2]

In addition to language, these attributes include food, clothing, tools and technologies, and religious beliefs and ceremonies. Maize continues to be the primary staple among present-day Nahuas, and they prepare it much as their ancestors did, as tortillas, tamales, *atolli* (a maize porridge) and right off the cob just before harvest when the maize is especially tender and sweet. Vegetables and fruits such as several varieties of beans, squashes and chillies are important supplements to the diet, as in past centuries. Turkeys and their eggs are also consumed, as is honey from stingless bees. *Pulque* is a popular drink, often available in markets. These and other foods derive from ancient times in Mesoamerica, but the present-day Nahua diet also draws on introductions such as rice, fruits such as oranges and limes, chickens and their eggs, coffee, sugarcane, and spices such as cloves and black pepper. Wheat bread is uncommonly substituted for maize tortillas. A traditional diet based on maize continues to be preferred, especially in rural areas.

Nahua clothing is distinctive. Often an individual can be identified by the designs on items of traditional clothing, especially women's blouses, capes and belts. Depending on the region, women's clothing consists of a wrap-around skirt with a colourful belt and either an indigenous style *huipilli* (tunic) or a *quechquemitl* (triangular-shaped cape) draped over a Spanish-style blouse. In the Sierra Norte de Puebla, a woman dressing up for a festive event wears a black wool wrap-around skirt, a white embroidered blouse, an embroidered *quechquemitl* and a dramatic headpiece constructed of purple and green wool coils covered by another *quechquemitl*.[3] Men's 'Indian clothing' consists of loose-fitting trousers and shirts. Interestingly, 'Indian clothing' today for both men and women is a combination of native elements and Spanish materials and styles, persisting together to the present day. This blending began in the sixteenth century. Despite these continuities, today many Nahua men, women and children wear Western-style clothing such as dresses, plaid shirts, jeans and flip-flops.

Although a great many objects and tools have entered indigenous communities over the years since the Spanish arrival, many

The author examines a hand-woven textile with the weaver and her friends.
A woman is dressed up in her finest for a festive occasion.

native households continue to possess and use tools and technologies deriving from ancient times. The Nahua woman seen here stands by one of her most treasured possessions, a backstrap loom. Although less and less common, women do continue this ancient activity, essentially transforming a bundle of sticks into a complex tool for producing cloth. Likewise, women continue to spin thread on hand spindles. In both cases, wool as well as cotton are spun and woven by hand, although the spinning and weaving of maguey fibres is barely done today. Sometimes synthetic threads are purchased in the market and woven at home on backstrap looms. Other traditional tools and technologies persisting from pre-Columbian times include the ubiquitous stone *mano* and *metate* for grinding maize, wooden dibble sticks and hoes (most now steel-tipped) for planting crops, and the cultivation of *chinampa* fields utilizing ancient methods (although now crops are selected based on modern urban consumer demands and produce is transported to market in trucks).

One of the most tenacious elements of indigenous culture that continues today throughout central Mexico is the nearly universal periodic market system. This is an ancient institution, pre-dating the Aztecs themselves. Its continued and widespread vitality is certainly due, in large part, to its efficiency in distributing goods and services (and news and rumour) within and across regions. These markets (today called *tianguiz*, from Nahuatl *tianquiztli*) offer daily and weekly necessities from food and firewood to clothing and pots. Markets were (and are) sensitive to seasonal cycles, with an abundance of maize at harvest time and overflowing with flowers prior to a highly anticipated ceremony. A time-travelling Aztec family could easily navigate one of these twenty-first-century markets, seeing merchandise grouped by type and people bargaining for the best prices, and occasionally using barter in their transactions. They would have recognized ceramic cookware, gorgeous and aromatic flowers, and all kinds of vegetables laid out on mats by household vendors selling small lots of their own surpluses. They would enjoy the aroma of the street food sizzling on a cook's griddle. But they would have been jolted by displays of blue jeans, white trousers and an array of colourful shirts (but no loincloths or capes); and by boots, candles, colourful plastic pans, drinks in glass bottles, batteries, CDs, spools of synthetically dyed threads and plastic bags. They would have figured out that coins and paper money have replaced their cacao beans and cotton cloths as forms of currency. A tourist snapping pictures would have struck a discordant note. Our Aztec time-travellers would have trekked to the market on foot, carrying their wares and purchases on their backs, as many native market-goers do today. But many also travel by bus, the fumes of which would surely assault the senses of our anachronistic Aztec family. In place of long merchant caravans, they observe trucks that have now expanded the marketing scale and geographic range of entrepreneurs, some of whom travel considerable distances for anticipated economic gain (as did the Aztec *pochteca*, but on foot).

Elements of native religion persist to the present day and permeate Nahua culture in a wide range of beliefs and rituals. These include 'a pantheon of spirit entities' that are 'personifications of water, clouds, rain, earth, sacred hills, sun, seeds, fire, death, and a host of underworld figures';[4] beliefs in animal companion spirits and transforming sorcerers; beliefs in omens, evil spirits and disease-causing winds; rituals involving the cutting of paper images and

Herbal medicines for sale in a marketplace.

offerings of copal incense, flowers and tobacco; rituals based on the life cycle of maize; divination and curing rituals; the identification of sacred sites; and pilgrimages to locations with special sacred power, especially mountains, caves and springs. These many beliefs and rituals exist within the contours of Christianity. Nearly five hundred years of contact, conflict and accommodation have resulted in perhaps unexpected but understandable religious retentions, blendings and transformations. There are a multitude of examples beyond those mentioned in Chapter Ten. For instance, to the Nahua of Tepoztlan, Morelos, 'the Catholic Trinity is viewed as a combination of three distinct gods, and the cross is a magical symbol which has no relation to the death of Jesus. Tepoztecans continue to fear omens, evil spirits, and *los aires*.'[5]

Hybrids like these are everyday and commonplace, and permeate every aspect of Nahua culture: a woman in a Western-style dress grinds maize on a *metate*, a woman in native dress asks for vitamin pills, a man goes to church to have his crops' seeds blessed by a priest, Coke and Pepsi sit alongside *atolli* and tamales on Day of the Dead altars, and in the homes of the Nahua of the Huasteca in eastern Mexico paper images of spirits hang alongside pictures of Catholic saints.[6] Beyond these historic fusions, Nahua living in both rural and urban settings are increasingly entwined in today's highly globalized world with all of its technological and other complexities. I am reminded of an interview I had with a Nahua shaman: when my tape recorder malfunctioned and I couldn't get it running again, he fiddled with it and, without any fuss, easily got it started. A bit further north, in the Huasteca, Nahua use telephones, television, computers and email. They have their own highly appropriate Nahuatl words for these. For instance, email is *tepozmecaixtlatiltlahcuilloli* (apparatus where writing is delivered to your face) and television is *tepoztezcatlamomolincacopincayotl* (apparatus where the drawings move themselves on the mirror [glass]).[7] The Nahua, over many centuries, have been adept at creatively maintaining their language and valued traditions, at the same time adjusting to new and unfamiliar situations.

More Cultural Continuations and Revivals

The Aztec imprint on the modern world (in Mexico and beyond) can be seen in language use, in material things and as potent symbols. In addition to its 2 million speakers, the Nahuatl language lives today in innumerable place names throughout Mexico. Most of the towns, cities and major landscape features discussed in this book are called today by (usually) Hispanicized versions of their Nahuatl names. So ancient Otompan is today's Otumba, Tochtepec is Tuxtepec, Tlacopan is Tacuba, Tlaxcalla is Tlaxcala, Huaxacac is Oaxaca, and Tepoztlan is Tepoztlán; Xochimilco is still Xochimilco, and Popocatepetl (Smoking Mountain) also retains its Nahuatl name. Mexico (the country) and Mexico (the city) derive from 'Mexica'. Following the pattern of Spanish-Nahuatl combinations already mentioned, many Nahuatl place names are preceded by a Spanish name, usually that of a saint. For example, since colonial times the four major quarters of Mexico City have been known as San Juan Moyotlan, San Pablo Teopan, San Sebastián Atzacoalco, and Santa María la Redonda Cuepopan.

Beyond place names, the Nahuatl names of many plants, animals, foods and specific objects are embedded in Spanish and other languages. Notable among these that have worked their way into English (usually through Spanish) are tomato (Nahuatl *xitomatl* or *tomatl*), avocado (*ahuacatl*), cacao (*cacahuatl*), chilli or chile (*chilli*), guacamole (*ahuacamolli*), tamale (*tamalli*) and coyote (*coyotl*). Mexican cuisine, based largely on pre-Columbian foods, is popular around the world, although usually tweaked to fit into local dietary preferences and conventions. Pre-Columbian dietary delights have penetrated some particularly interesting venues: for instance, Safeco Field, home of the Seattle Mariners' baseball team, offers to its fans bags of ancient Mexico-inspired *chapulines* (toasted grasshoppers flavoured with lime and chilli).

Some of the primary cultural, political and religious symbols of Mexico draw on indigenous elements. The national seal and flag feature the Aztec eagle-snake-cactus symbolism. The Virgin of Guadalupe, a national religious symbol of Mexico, fuses the Virgin Mary and the Aztec goddess Tonantzin. An imposing statue of

Mexican flag with eagle, serpent and cactus.

Cuauhtemoc presides over one of Mexico City's busiest intersections. Mexico's National Palace features magnificent murals with compelling Aztec imagery.[8] Ruins of ancient cities of the Aztecs and their predecessors can be seen all over the Mexican landscape – famous sites such as Teotihuacan (Classic period), Tula (Early Postclassic), and Malinalco, Tlatelolco and Tenochtitlan (Late Postclassic/Aztec period) evoke past histories; their physical reality gives substance to ancient and modern identities. Since 1978, ground-breaking excavations in the heart of Mexico City (old Tenochtitlan) have gained worldwide recognition for their meticulous procedures and extraordinary discoveries. Additionally, archaeological excavations at sites throughout Mexico often directly involve people from local communities, firmly tying them to their past heritages.

On the global stage, the Museo Nacional de Antropología and Museo Templo Mayor, both in Mexico City, are internationally renowned. Mexico presented the 'Aztec Palace' at the 1889 Exposition Universelle in Paris, tying the Mexican past to the broader modern world. In the United States, many Mexican-Americans associate with Aztlan, the real or mythical place of origin of the Aztecs. According to Davíd Carrasco, 'Central to this vision is the lineage that Chicanos claim goes back to the "northern land of Aztlan", the place of emergence of the Aztec ancestors' and 'Today, Aztlan is used as a name for community centers, parks, and nicknames wherever Mexican-Americans live.'[9] On a less positive note, 'Montezuma's Revenge' refers to intestinal discomfort suffered by tourists visiting Mexico (or sometimes generalized to refer to similar experiences elsewhere); the name also refers to a video game and a rollercoaster at Knott's Berry Farm in California (appropriately tweaked to 'Montezooma's Revenge').

The Aztecs of the Imagination

Mere mention of the Aztecs continues to stir the modern imagination. They are often incorporated into all manner of the arts and popular culture, including films, television programmes, video games, comic books, dances, books, design and fashion. Examples are legion – here are but a few. Ballet Folklorico performances are extremely popular in Mexico and beyond. Books seeking an exotic culture and storyline are sometimes built around the Aztecs (for instance, *Scooby Doo! The Mystery of the Aztec Tomb*), and the tongue-in-cheek Horrible Histories series of books includes the *Angry Aztecs*. *Pirates of the Caribbean: The Curse of the Black Pearl* (2003) features rather un-Aztec 'Aztec gold pieces'. Producers have been moved numerous times to include Aztec gods and goddesses (or entities with their names) in popular movies and TV shows (including *Stargate SG-1* episodes), video and other popular games (such as *Indiana Jones and the Infernal Machine* and *Dungeons and Dragons*), and comic books (including *Wonder Woman*). Some of these perpetuate stereotypes, but good documentaries such as *Engineering an Empire* seek a balanced presentation of the Aztecs. Furthermore, a team of modern scientists has named our Sun 'mother star' after Coatlicue, an Aztec mother goddess.[10]

In the world of design, fashion and crafts, it is not uncommon to find modern fabric designs, especially colourful geometrics, dubbed 'Aztec', whether based on documented Aztec designs or not. But more to the point, some native people have smartly worked themselves into the modern world of design, as have the people of the small Otomí village of San Pablito, Hidalgo. This village has become famous for its colourful embroideries of fanciful creatures and graceful plants. These wondrous embroideries work their way

A modern Otomí woman sells popular embroideries in a marketplace.

well beyond their local marketplaces; I have seen one creatively stretched into a lampshade, and have found a large embroidered textile for sale in the gift shop of the Victoria and Albert Museum in London. A related craft undertaken by people in many communities produces paintings on native paper (*amate*, Nahuatl *amatl*) – again with flowing plants but with somewhat more realistic animals.[11] Similarly, native woodcarvings sometimes exhibit global themes – in the 1970s I found a native woodcarver who expertly fashioned his local woods into traditional objects, but also an elephant or two. Whether embroidered on cloth, painted on paper or carved in wood, the imagery is whimsical and imaginative, and eminently marketable.

A sixteenth-century image of an eagle perched on a cactus, celebrating the founding of the Mexica city of Tenochtitlan, appears early in this book. The book approaches its end with almost the same imagery on the twenty-first-century Mexican flag. The past is present. This 'lost civilization' is not so lost after all.

MONTH	DATES	PRIMARY DEITY	RELIGIOUS THEME(S)
1 Atl cauatl	13 Feb. – 4 Mar.	Chalchiuhtlicue, Tlaloque (Tlaloc minions)	Rain and agricultural fertility
2 Tlacaxipehualiztli	5 Mar. – 24 Mar.	Xipe Totec	Rain and agricultural fertility
3 Toçoztontli	25 Mar. – 13 Apr.	Chalchiuhtlicue, Tlaloque, Centeotl (maize)	Rain and agricultural fertility
4 Huey toçoztli	14 Apr. – 3 May	Tlaloque, Centeotl, Quetzalcoatl	Rain and agricultural fertility
5 Toxcatl	4 May – 23 May	Tezcatlipoca, Huitzilopochtli	Celestial creativity, war
6 Etzalcualiztli	24 May – 12 June	Tlaloc, Chalchiuhtlicue, Quetzalcoatl	Rain and agricultural fertility
7 Tecuilhuitontli	13 June – 2 July	Xochipilli	Rain and agricultural fertility
8 Huey tecuilhuitl	3 July – 22 July	Cihuacoatl (mother goddess), Xilonen (maize)	Rain and agricultural fertility
9 Tlaxochimaco	23 July – 11 Aug.	Tezcatlipoca, Huitzilopochtli	Celestial creativity, war
10 Xocotl uetzi	12 Aug. – 31 Aug.	Xiuhtecuhtli (fire god)	Celestial creativity
11 Ochpaniztli	1 Sept. – 20 Sept.	Teteoinan (mother goddess), Centeotl	Rain and agricultural fertility
12 Teotl eco	21 Sept. – 10 Oct.	Tezcatlipoca, Huitzilopochtli	Celestial creativity, war
13 Tepeilhuitl	11 Oct. – 30 Oct.	Tlaloque, Xochiquetzal	Rain and agricultural fertility
14 Quecholli	31 Oct. – 19 Nov.	Mixcoatl-Camaxtli	War
15 Panquetzaliztli	20 Nov. – 9 Dec.	Tezcatlipoca, Huitzilopochtli	Celestial creativity, war
16 Atemoztli	10 Dec. – 29 Dec.	Tlaloque	Rain and agricultural fertility
17 Tititl	30 Dec. – 18 Jan.	Cihuacoatl	Rain and agricultural fertility
18 Izcalli	19 Jan. – 7 Feb.	Xiuhtecuhtli	Celestial creativity
Nemontemi	8 Feb. – 12 Feb.	——	Barren days

REFERENCES

Introduction

1 Benjamin Keen, *The Aztec Image in Western Thought* (New Brunswick, NJ, 1971), p. 69.
2 See Deborah L. Nichols, 'The Rural and Urban Landscapes of the Aztec State', in *Mesoamerican Archaeology: Theory and Practice*, ed. Julia A. Hendon and Rosemary A. Joyce (Oxford, 2004), pp. 265–95.
3 See especially Sabine Haag, Alfonso de Maria y Campos, Lilia Rivero Weber and Christian Feest, eds, *El Penacho del México Antiguo* (Altenstadt, 2012).

1 'An Enchanted Vision'

1 Bernal Díaz del Castillo, *The History of the Conquest of New Spain*, ed. Davíd Carrasco (Albuquerque, NM, 2008), p. 156. Bernal Díaz styled his history as the 'true' history of the conquest.
2 This was not an army and these were not soldiers in the modern sense of the term. They were not technically men-at-arms, but rather men-with-arms.
3 Among the company were two friars, several notaries, a doctor, half a dozen carpenters and at least fifty sailors, as well as men who had been miners, mechanics and musicians in earlier lives.
4 Edwin Place and Herbert Behm, eds, *Amadis of Gaul, Books I and II* (Lexington, KY, 2003), vol. I, p. 113. In the late fifteenth century the Spanish writer Garci Rodríguez de Montalvo worked on these stories in Bernal Díaz's hometown of Medina del Campo while this future conquistador was growing up there.
5 Díaz del Castillo, *The History of the Conquest*, p. xxviii.
6 These analyses of the map are based primarily on Barbara Mundy, 'Mapping the Aztec Capital: The 1524 Nuremberg Map of Tenochtitlan, Its Sources and Meaning', *Imago Mundi*, 50 (1998), pp. 11–33, and Elizabeth Hill Boone, 'This New World Now Revealed: Hernán Cortés and the Presentation of Mexico to Europe', *Word and Image*, XXVII/1 (2011),

pp. 31–46. Matthew Restall, in *When Moctezuma Met Cortés* (New York, 2018), p. 117, suggests it was made in Seville by a Spanish engraver.

7 Anonymous Conqueror, 'The Chronicle of the Anonymous Conqueror', in *The Conquistadors*, ed. P. de Fuentes (Norman, OK, 1963), p. 167; Hernando Cortés, *5 Letters of Cortés to the Emperor*, ed. J. Bayard Morris (New York, 1928), p. 132.

8 This is the still-active Popocatepetl, at the southeastern edge of the Basin. The highest mountain in Mesoamerica is the volcanic Pico de Orizaba, or Citlaltepetl, at 5,636 metres (18,491 ft).

9 Díaz del Castillo, *The History of the Conquest*, p. 71.

10 The Moors were defeated by Ferdinand and Isabella in the *Reconquista* of 1492.

11 The *Codex Mendoza*, fol. 71v. See Frances F. Berdan and Patricia Rieff Anawalt, *The Codex Mendoza*, 4 vols (Berkeley, CA, 1992).

12 Anonymous Conqueror, 'The Chronicle of the Anonymous Conqueror', p. 168.

13 Díaz del Castillo, *The History of the Conquest*, pp. 165–6.

14 Francisco de Aguilar, 'The Chronicle of Fray Francisco de Aguilar', in *The Conquistadors*, ed. P. de Fuentes, p. 147. Aguilar guarded Motecuhzoma during his captivity under the Spaniards in Tenochtitlan and penned his account later, in 1560.

15 Patrick Thomas Hajovsky, 'André Thevet's "True" Portrait of Moctezuma and its European Legacy', *Word and Image*, XXV/4 (2009), p. 341.

2 WHO WERE THE AZTECS?

1 The *Codex Mendoza*, fol. 1r. See Frances F. Berdan and Patricia Rieff Anawalt, *The Codex Mendoza*, 4 vols (Berkeley, CA, 1992).

2 Davide Domenici, Constanza Miliani and Antonio Sgamellotti, 'Cultural and Historical Implications of Non-destructive Analyses on Mesoamerican Codices in the Bodleian Libraries', in *Mesoamerican Manuscripts*, ed. Maarten E.R.G.N. Jansen, Virginia M. Lladó-Buisán and Ludo Snijders (Leiden, 2019), pp. 160–74. Orpiment is arsenic trisulphide, a brilliant yellow.

3 Areas near these ancient sites, carrying their same names, continued to be inhabited through to the present day.

4 Teotihuacan is the name the Mexica and their contemporaries used to refer to the site. We do not know the name of this city at its height.

5 See Leonardo López Luján, *The Offerings of the Templo Mayor of Tenochtitlan* (Albuquerque, NM, 2005).

6 These include relief-sculpture banquettes and *chacmool* sculptures (reclining deity figures with receptacles for hearts) as well as ceramic vessels. Rather than deriving directly from Tula, Toltec-style objects in Tenochtitlan were more likely Mexica copies; see Emily Umberger, 'Antiques, Revivals, and References to the Past in Aztec Art', *RES,* 13 (1987), pp. 62–105.

7 The several migration histories tell roughly the same story. Elizabeth Boone, *Stories in Red and Black* (Austin, TX, 2000), pp. 213–21, provides an excellent discussion of these annals.

8 This is one version of the myth recounting the creation of the Mexica's Fifth Sun, or current world. See Chapter Nine.

9 This was begun in 1418, destroyed by a flood in 1449 and replaced by a new and improved version. The Mexica drew on existing knowledge and technologies, developed as many as 1,500 years earlier; see Frances F. Berdan, *Aztec Archaeology and Ethnohistory* (Cambridge, 2014), pp. 78–9.

10 Frederic Hicks, 'Ethnicity', in *The Oxford Encyclopedia of Mesoamerican Cultures*, ed. Davíd Carrasco (Oxford, 2001), vol. I, pp. 388–92, enumerates 27 distinctive ethnic groups in the Basin of Mexico.

11 For an expanded discussion of Aztec ethnicity, see Frances F. Berdan, 'Concepts of Ethnicity and Class in Aztec-period Mexico', in Frances F. Berdan et al., *Ethnic Identity in Nahua Mesoamerica* (Salt Lake City, UT, 2008), pp. 105–32.

3 Building an Empire

1 The *Codex Mendoza*, fol. 11v. See Frances F. Berdan and Patricia Rieff Anawalt, *The Codex Mendoza*, 4 vols (Berkeley, CA, 1992).

2 *Códice Chimalpopoca* (Mexico City, 1975), p. 67; Berdan and Anawalt, *The Codex Mendoza*, vol. II, pp. 20–21.

3 Diego Durán, *The History of the Indies of New Spain*, ed. Doris Heyden (Norman, OK, 1994), p. 307.

4 Excellent descriptions and interpretations of this Tenochtitlan masterpiece include Esther Pasztory, *Aztec Art* (New York, 1983), pp. 147–50, and Emily Umberger, 'Ethnicity and Other Identities in the Sculptures of Tenochtitlan', in *Ethnic Identity in Nahua Mesoamerica*, ed. Frances F. Berdan et al. (Salt Lake City, UT, 2008), pp. 64–104. The Tizoc Stone's colourful history is unravelled by Alfredo López Austin and Leonardo López Luján in 'The Posthumous History of the Tizoc Stone', in *Fanning the Sacred Flame*, ed. Matthew A. Boxt and Brian Dervin Dillon (Louisville, CO, 2012), pp. 439–60. This massive sculpted stone was unearthed in 1790, along with two other Classic Mexica monuments, the Calendar Stone and the statue of Coatlicue. All three currently anchor the Mexica Hall of the Museo Nacional de Antropología in Mexico City.

5 Emily Umberger, 'Tezcatlipoca and Huitzilopochtli: Political Dimensions of Aztec Deities', in *Tezcatlipoca: Trickster and Supreme Deity*, ed. Elizabeth Baquedano (Boulder, CO, 2014), pp. 83–112.

6 This layering of the cosmic world was a popular motif among the Aztecs, and was repeated over and over again in the buried offerings around Tenochtitlan's ceremonial precinct.

7 Motecuhzoma Xocoyotzin died in 1520 during the chaos of the Spanish incursion. He was succeeded by Cuitlahuac, who died six months later

of smallpox. His successor, Cuauhtemoc, was captured by the Spaniards on 13 August 1521, marking the end of the war in Tenochtitlan.

8 A few chroniclers, most notably Diego Durán, place an additional figure, Tlacaelel, on the Mexica political pedestal. His official title was *Cihuacoatl* (Woman-snake). He served as second-in-command to the Tenochtitlan ruler, and is glorified as the force behind the throne in the Mexica's bid for political and military supremacy. The extent of his powers remains controversial.

9 The term 'provinces' refers specifically to the groupings of conquered city-states laid out in the *Codex Mendoza*. Most provinces were ethnically and linguistically diverse. See Frances F. Berdan et al., *Aztec Imperial Strategies* (Washington, DC, 1996).

4 Making a Living in Country and City

1 Bernardino de Sahagún, *Florentine Codex*, ed. Arthur J. O. Anderson and Charles E. Dibble (Salt Lake City, UT, 1950–82), vol. X, pp. 41–2.

2 Ibid., p. 25.

3 Christian Feest, 'Mexican Featherwork in Austrian Habsburg Collections', in *Images Take Flight*, ed. Alessandra Russo, Gerhard Wolf and Diana Fane (Florence, 2015), pp. 290–97.

4 One resides in the Museo Nacional de Historia in Chapultepec Castle in Mexico City, two live in the Württembergisches Landesmuseum, Stuttgart, Germany, and this shield is housed in the Weltmuseum Wien, Austria. This description relies especially on the meticulous work of Renée Riedler, 'Materials and Technique of the Feather Shield Preserved in Vienna', in *Images Take Flight*, ed. Russo, Wolf and Fane, pp. 330–41. I also rely on the work of Filloy Nadal and Moreno Guzmán, cited in note 5.

5 This is the feather shield in Chapultepec Castle in Mexico City, and the count is the result of the tireless research of Laura Filloy Nadal and María Olvido Moreno Guzmán, 'Precious Feathers and Fancy Fifteenth-century Feathered Shields', in *Rethinking the Aztec Economy*, ed. Deborah L. Nichols, Frances F. Berdan and Michael E. Smith (Tucson, AZ, 2017), pp. 156–94.

6 Frances F. Berdan and Patricia Rieff Anawalt, *The Codex Mendoza*, 4 vols (Berkeley, CA, 1992), vol. III, fol. 65r.

7 See Guilhem Olivier, *Mockeries and Metamorphoses of an Aztec God* (Boulder, CO, 2003).

8 Frances F. Berdan, *Aztec Archaeology and Ethnohistory* (Cambridge, 2014), p. 79.

9 An annual consumption of an estimated 900,000–1,000,000 ducks is recorded for the Basin of Mexico in the eighteenth century, a time when these resources were diminished from pre-Spanish times; Charles Gibson, *The Aztecs under Spanish Rule* (Stanford, CA, 1964), p. 343.

10 Some estimates reach as high as 2,560,000 items annually. I prefer the more conservative number, which is still impressive. Berdan and Anawalt, *The Codex Mendoza*, vol. I, pp. 154–6.

11 Alyson M. Thibodeau et al., 'Was Aztec and Mixtec Turquoise Mined in the American Southwest?', *Science Advances*, 4/6 eaas9370 (13 June 2018).

12 The disc was discovered in the early 1900s in a cave in the vicinity of Tehuacan in central Mexico. Along with several other mosaic discs and masks, the artefact now resides in the National Museum of the American Indian, Smithsonian Institution, Washington, DC.

13 Berdan, *Aztec Archaeology and Ethnohistory*, p. 92.

5 Markets and Merchants

1 Peter Martyr D'Anghera, *De Orbo Novo*, trans. Francis Augustus MacNutt (New York, 1912), vol. II, pp. 354–6. The original was written in Latin and first published in 1516.

2 More details on cacao and its tree can be found in Allen Young, *The Chocolate Tree: A Natural History of Cacao* (Gainesville, FL, 2007) and Sophie D. Coe and Michael D. Coe, *The True History of Chocolate* (London, 1996).

3 This is recorded in a 1545 document from Tlaxcalla in Arthur J. O. Anderson et al., *Beyond the Codices* (Berkeley, CA, 1976), pp. 208–13.

4 Motolinía [Fray Toribio de Benavente], *Memoriales o libro de las cosas de la Nueva España y de los naturales de ella*, ed. E. O'Gorman (Mexico City, 1971), p. 367.

5 See Dorothy Hosler, 'Metal Production', in *The Postclassic Mesoamerican World*, ed. Michael E. Smith and Frances F. Berdan (Salt Lake City, UT, 2003), pp. 159–71.

6 Diego de Landa, *Relación de las Cosas de Yucatan*, trans. Alfred M. Tozzer (Cambridge, MA, 1941), pp. 94–6.

7 Bernal Díaz del Castillo, *The History of the Conquest of New Spain*, ed. Davíd Carrasco (Albuquerque, NM, 2008), p. 175.

8 As reported in 'The Chronicle of the Anonymous Conqueror', in *The Conquistadors*, ed. P. de Fuentes (Norman, OK, 1963), pp. 178–9. Hernando Cortés, 5 *Letters of Cortés to the Emperor*, ed. J. Bayard Morris (New York, 1928), p. 87, suggests that 60,000 buyers and sellers attended that market daily.

9 Díaz del Castillo, *The History of the Conquest*, p. 174.

10 This is found in Bernardino de Sahagún's *Florentine Codex*, ed. Arthur J. O. Anderson and Charles E. Dibble (Salt Lake City, UT, 1950–82), vol. VIII, pp. 67–9. Markets were remarkably persistent, continuing to flourish after the transformation of Aztec Mexico into Spanish New Spain.

11 Ibid., vol. X, pp. 66–7.

12 Canoe traffic on the open sea hugged the coastlines. The native Americans did not make or use sails.

13 Sahagún, *Florentine Codex*, vol. IX, p. 13. *Pinole* (*pinolli* in Nahuatl) is ground roasted maize, often mixed with flavourings such as cacao, vanilla or chia seeds.

14 Frances F. Berdan, *Aztec Archaeology and Ethnohistory* (Cambridge, 2014), p. 188.
15 This was Columbus's fourth voyage to the Americas.
16 Diego Durán, *Book of the Gods and Rites and the Ancient Calendar*, ed. and trans. Fernando Horcasitas and Doris Heyden (Norman, OK, 1971), p. 278.

6 NOBLES AND COMMONERS

1 Diego Durán, *Book of the Gods and Rites and the Ancient Calendar*, ed. and trans. Fernando Horcasitas and Doris Heyden (Norman, OK, 1971), p. 196.
2 In Texcoco, sons succeeded fathers; in Tenochtitlan, brothers tended to succeed brothers.
3 Durán, *The History of the Indies of New Spain*, ed. Doris Heyden (Norman, OK, 1994), pp. 208–10.
4 James Lockhart, *The Nahuas after the Conquest* (Stanford, CA, 1992), p. 96.
5 Bernardino de Sahagún, *Florentine Codex*, ed. Arthur J. O. Anderson and Charles E. Dibble (Salt Lake City, UT, 1950–82), vol. IV, p. 124.
6 Frances F. Berdan, *Aztec Archaeology and Ethnohistory* (Cambridge, 2014), pp. 63–4, 183.
7 Fernando Alvarado Tezozomoc, *Crónica Mexicana* (Mexico City, 1975), pp. 668–9.
8 Sahagún, *Florentine Codex*, vol. IV, p. 5.
9 Motolinía [Fray Toribio de Benavente], *Memoriales o libro de las cosas de la Nueva España y de los naturales de ella*, ed. E. O'Gorman (Mexico City, 1971), p. 367.
10 This day arrived every 260 days.

7 TO BE A PROPER AZTEC

1 Bernardino de Sahagún, *Florentine Codex*, ed. Arthur J. O. Anderson and Charles E. Dibble (Salt Lake City, UT, 1950–82), vol. VI, p. 125.
2 Ibid., p. 123.
3 A woman's reputation often rested on the quality of her textile work. I am reminded of an incident in a small Nahua village in the Sierra Norte de Puebla, Mexico: I had purchased a hand-woven garment at one house, and later, a woman from another household grabbed it and berated me for buying it, immediately identifying the weaver and stating in no uncertain terms that everyone knew that this woman's work was 'shoddy and worthless'. What was I thinking?
4 Sahagún, *Florentine Codex*, vol. X, pp. 178–9, 193, 259.
5 Ibid., p. 51.
6 Ibid., vol. IV, pp. 5, 7, 10–13, 19–21, 23–4, 30, 34, 41–5. This is just a sampling. The entirety of Book 4 is devoted to these day name meanings.
7 Diego Durán, *Book of the Gods and Rites and the Ancient Calendar*, ed. Fernando Horcasitas and Doris Heyden (Norman, OK, 1971), p. 424.

This was the second of the Mexica kings named Motecuhzoma. We do not know the genesis of the earlier Motecuhzoma's name, and it is entirely possible that the second was simply named after the first. But for Durán, at least it made a good story.

8 Apologies to Beatrix Potter.

9 Frances F. Berdan and Patricia Rieff Anawalt, *The Codex Mendoza* (Berkeley, CA, 1992), vol. III, fols 57v–60r.

10 See Frances F. Berdan, *Aztec Archaeology and Ethnohistory* (Cambridge, 2014), p. 307.

11 Sahagún, *Florentine Codex*, vol. VIII, p. 72.

12 This is in contrast to warfare and ritual human sacrifice which, while violent, were institutionalized. Homicide was not.

13 For instance, a fraudulant bean seller mixed infested beans with good ones, and a deceiving metal seller 'cleaned up' his objects so they looked better than they really were. Cacao bean counterfeiters are well documented. See Sahagún, *Florentine Codex*, vol. X, pp. 66, 61.

14 This is reminiscent of English women handing white feathers to men who they thought should be enlisting in the First World War.

8 SCIENCE, MEDICINE AND LIFE'S PRACTICALITIES

1 Anonymous Conqueror, 'The Chronicle of the Anonymous Conqueror', in *The Conquistadors,* ed. P. de Fuentes (Norman, OK, 1963), p. 173.

2 Jeffrey R. Parsons and Mary H. Parsons, *Maguey Utilization in Highland Central Mexico* (Ann Arbor, MI, 1990), p. 336. Cutting of leaves for fibres can happen during earlier stages of development. This book is an excellent source on maguey cultivation in central Mexico, past and present.

3 These details largely derive from observations of present-day maguey production; archaeological findings suggest strong parallels between past and present.

4 'It appears that in most *tierra fría* contexts maguey can produce approximately as many calories and essential nutrients per hectare as the standard seed crops; when the plant's flesh and sap are both consumed, maguey can potentially produce more calories than seed crops on a given unit of land'; Jeffrey R. Parsons, 'The Pastoral Niche in Pre-Hispanic Mesoamerica', in *Pre-Columbian Foodways*, ed. John E. Staller and Michael Carrasco (New York, 2010), p. 117.

5 Bernardino de Sahagún, *Florentine Codex*, ed. Arthur J. O. Anderson and Charles E. Dibble (Salt Lake City, UT, 1950–82), vol. VI, pp. 237, 238–40.

6 Matthew Restall, *When Montezuma Met Cortés* (New York, 2018), p. 130.

7 Andrés de Tapia, 'The Chronicle of Andrés de Tapia', in *The Conquistadors*, ed. P. de Fuentes, p. 40. His 'lions' and 'tigers' derived from his Spanish point of reference.

8 Diego Durán, *The History of the Indies of New Spain*, trans. Doris Heyden (Norman, OK, 1994), pp. 244–5.

9 Marshall Saville, *The Goldsmith's Art in Ancient Mexico* (New York, 1920), p. 119.

10 Motolinía [Fray Toribio de Benavente], *Motolinía's History of the Indians of New Spain* (New York, 1950), p. 241.

11 This implement can be seen on the bottom right of the illustration of the founding of Tenochtitlan in Berdan and Anawalt, *The Codex Mendoza* (Berkeley, CA, 1992), vol. III, fol 2r.

12 Juan de Torquemada, *Monarquía Indiana* (Mexico City, 1969), vol. I, p. 188. Translation in Miguel León-Portilla, *Aztec Thought and Culture* (Norman, OK, 1963), p. 142.

13 Anthony F. Aveni, 'Mesoamerican Calendars and Archaeoastronomy', in *The Oxford Handbook of Mesoamerican Archaeology*, ed. Deborah L. Nichols and Christopher A. Pool (Oxford, 2012), pp. 787–8.

14 Good information on these matters can be found in Bernard Ortiz de Montellano, *Aztec Medicine, Health and Nutrition* (New Brunswick, NJ, 1990), and Juan Alberto Román Berrelleza, 'Health and Disease among the Aztecs', in *The Aztec World*, ed. Elizabeth M. Brumfiel and Gary M. Feinman (New York, 2008), pp. 53–65.

15 Frances F. Berdan and Patricia Rieff Anawalt, *The Codex Mendoza* (Berkeley, CA, 1992), vol. IV, fol. 71r.

16 Sahagún, *Florentine Codex*, vol. X, p. 30.

17 Ibid., vol. VI, pp. 156–7.

18 Frances F. Berdan and Michael E. Smith, *Everyday Life in the Aztec World* (Cambridge, 2021), discusses midwives and midwifery in some detail.

19 Leonardo López Luján, *The Offerings of the Templo Mayor of Tenochtitlan* (Albuquerque, NM, 2005).

9 Gods, Sacrifice and the Meaning of Life

1 John Bierhorst, *History and Mythology of the Aztecs: The Codex Chimalpopoca* (Tucson, AZ, 1992), pp. 145–6.

2 A classic article on Aztec religion is H. B. Nicholson's 'Religion in Pre-Hispanic Central Mexico' in *Handbook of Middle American Indians*, vol. X (Austin, TX, 1971), pp. 395–446.

3 Frances F. Berdan, *Aztec Archaeology and Ethnohistory* (Cambridge, 2014), p. 219.

4 In Nahuatl, *centzontli* (400) also means 'many'.

5 This city-state was about 72 km (45 mi.) southwest of Tenochtitlan. It was conquered by Axayacatl (r. 1468–81).

6 This does not correspond to the Christian hell, since it carried no moral value.

7 There would have been noticeable differences in these offerings according to social status: a high-ranking person would be accompanied on his journey by sacrificed slaves and other costly goods; a poor commoner family could afford only humble offerings.

8   Good descriptions of these rites and their implications are found in Richard Townsend, *The Aztecs* (London, 2000), pp. 140–45, and H. B. Nicholson, 'The Annual "Royal Ceremony" on Mt. Tlaloc: Mountain Fertility Ritualism in the Late Pre-Hispanic Basin of Mexico', in *Mesas and Cosmologies in Mesoamerica*, ed. Douglas Sharon (San Diego, CA, 2003), pp. 33–49.

9   In addition to heart removal, persons destined for sacrifice might be otherwise dispatched depending on the ceremony, for example by being shot with arrows or thrown into a fire.

10 Musical instruments included conch shells, drums, whistles or flutes, rattles and bone rasps.

11 It was recorded that Motecuhzoma Xocoyotzin made elaborate offerings of clothing, jewels, feathers and quail before heading off to battle, expecting godly favour in his military expedition.

12 A fine analysis of these offerings is Leonardo López Luján's *The Offerings of the Templo Mayor of Tenochtitlan* (Albuquerque, NM, 2005), and 'The Codex Mendoza and the Archaeology of Tenochtitlan', in *Mesoamerican Manuscripts*, ed. Maarten E.R.G.N. Jansen et al. (Leiden, 2019), pp. 15–44.

10   The End of the Fifth Age: The Setting Sun

1   In Miguel León-Portilla, *Aztec Thought and Culture* (Norman, OK, 1963), pp. 64–6. This quotation is part of a larger exchange, called *Coloquios*, set down in Nahuatl under the supervision of Bernardino de Sahagún in the 1560s.

2   It is not entirely clear if these were important priests, or scholars and philosophers.

3   The feather identifications on this object have not been scientifically established. Still, they can be suggested from identifications on other colonial feather mosaics. Hummingbirds were widespread, and local ducks possibly provided the brown and white feathers. The pink feathers were probably plucked from roseate spoonbills, the yellow feathers perhaps from the yellow-winged cacique, and the orange feathers possibly from the tail feathers of scarlet macaws; all of these birds lived in lowland habitats. If these identifications are correct, and the object was most likely fashioned in central Mexico, that means that lowland feathers were still available to highland featherworkers well into colonial times.

4   For example, the master featherworker fashioned each of his bricks individually and then set them together on the mosaic; the other two featherworkers laid out the bricks in strips, a less demanding technique.

5   The central panel measures 482 × 317 mm (19 × 12½ in.) and each side panel 482 × 159 mm (19 × 6¼ in.). Its early history is obscure, but at some point it came into a private Florentine collection, from where it was transferred to a Manhattan law firm (Coudert Brothers) that represented international investors. In 1888 the law firm gifted the object to the Metropolitan Museum of Art in New York City, where

it is housed today. A similar triptych lives today in the Museo Nacional de Arte in Mexico City.

6 Camilla Townsend, *Fifth Sun* (Oxford, 2019), p. 97.

7 Mystery still shrouds his death. The Spaniards had led him to the palace rooftop to speak to his infuriated populace: some argue that these people killed him with stones, others that the Spaniards killed him. He had been held hostage for about eighty days.

8 This is just a brief overview of these momentous events. Among the many detailed and historically sound accounts are Hugh Thomas, *Conquest* (New York, 1993) and Matthew Restall, *When Moctezuma Met Cortés* (New York, 2018).

9 Thomas, *Conquest*, pp. 528–9.

10 Michel R. Oudijk and Matthew Restall, 'Mesoamerican Conquistadors in the Sixteenth Century', in *Indian Conquistadors*, ed. Laura E. Matthew and Michel R. Oudijk (Norman, OK, 2007), p. 33.

11 Spanish firearms, steel swords and crossbows are often contrasted with native lances, bows and arrows, slings and clubs inset with obsidian blades. We should also mention Spanish horses and ferocious dogs, the latter greatly feared by the natives.

12 Susan Schroeder, 'Looking Back at the Conquest', in *Chipping Away on Earth*, ed. Eloise Quiñones Keber (Lancaster, CA, 1994), pp. 81–94.

13 Matthew Restall, *Seven Myths of the Spanish Conquest* (Oxford, 2003), p. 47.

14 Ibid., p. 48.

15 These royal replacements were decried by Chimalpahin, a native writer of the seventeenth century. See Schroeder, 'Looking Back at the Conquest', pp. 81–94.

16 Charles Gibson, *The Aztecs under Spanish Rule* (Stanford, CA, 1964), p. 138. Warfare, overwork, famine and dislocations also contributed to these losses.

17 Restall, *Seven Myths of the Spanish Conquest*, pp. 54–5.

18 Ibid., p. 52.

19 More details on these mergings are in James Lockhart, *The Nahuas after the Conquest* (Stanford, CA, 1992), pp. 203–60; Louise M. Burkhart, *Aztecs on Stage* (Norman, OK, 2011); and David Tavárez, *The Invisible War* (Stanford, CA, 2011).

11 THE AZTEC LEGACY: REALITY AND IMAGINATION

1 Statement made to the author by a Nahua weaver in the Sierra Norte de Puebla, Mexico, 1985.

2 See Alan R. Sandstrom, 'The Aztecs and their Descendants in the Contemporary World', in *The Oxford Handbook of the Aztecs* (Oxford, 2017), pp. 707–20. Many other indigenous groups still reside in the territory of the ancient Aztec empire. There are Otomí, Mixtec, Zapotec, Totonac, Huaxtec and many others who have

retained their native languages and other elements of their ancient, traditional cultures.

3 Girls begin to wear these when they are very young – these early coils are small and few, and they increase as the girl grows into a woman.

4 Sandstrom, 'The Aztecs and their Descendants in the Contemporary World', p. 714.

5 Oscar Lewis, *Life in a Mexican Village* (Urbana, IL, 1963), p. 256.

6 Alan R. Sandstrom, *Corn Is Our Blood* (Norman, OK, 1991), p. 254.

7 Literally, email reads as 'metal-vine-face or eye-deliver-direct object-writing-noun ending' and television reads as 'metal-mirror [glass]-direct object-reflexive movement-this, that-image or drawing-noun ending'. Alan R. Sandstrom, personal communication, 2019.

8 Called *History of Mexico* and executed by Diego Rivera, 1929–35.

9 Davíd Carrasco, 'Imagining a Place for Aztlan', in *The Aztec World*, ed. Elizabeth M. Brumfiel and Gary M. Feinman (New York, 2008), pp. 228, 229.

10 'Solar System Genealogy Revealed by Meteorites', *Science x*, 29 August 2012, https://phys.org, accessed 10 July 2020.

11 This craft has been around longer than the embroideries. Some paintings and cut-outs on native paper are created for local ritual (often curing) purposes; many others are produced for the express purpose of targeting a broader, often tourist market.

BIBLIOGRAPHY

Alvarado Tezozomoc, Fernando, *Crónica Mexicana* (Mexico City, 1975)
Anderson, Arthur J. O., Frances Berdan and James Lockhart, *Beyond the
  Codices* (Berkeley, CA, 1976)
Anonymous Conqueror, 'The Chronicle of the Anonymous Conqueror', in
  The Conquistadors, ed. and trans. P. de Fuentes (Norman, OK, 1963),
  pp. 165–81
Aveni, Anthony, 'Mesoamerican Calendars and Archaeoastronomy', in
  The Oxford Handbook of Mesoamerican Archaeology, ed. D. L. Nichols
  and C. A. Pool (Oxford, 2012), pp. 787–94
Berdan, Frances F., *Aztec Archaeology and Ethnohistory* (Cambridge, 2014)
—, 'Concepts of Ethnicity and Class in Aztec-period Mexico', in *Ethnic Identity
  in Nahua Mesoamerica* , ed. F. F. Berdan et al. (Salt Lake City, UT, 2008),
  pp. 105–32
—, et al., *Aztec Imperial Strategies* (Washington, DC, 1996)
—, and Patricia Rieff Anawalt, *The Codex Mendoza*, 4 vols (Berkeley, CA, 1992)
—, and Michael E. Smith, *Everyday Life in the Aztec World* (Cambridge, 2021)
Bierhorst, John, *History and Mythology of the Aztecs: The Codex Chimalpopoca*
  (Tucson, AZ, 1992)
Boone, Elizabeth Hill, *Stories in Red and Black* (Austin, TX, 2000)
—, 'This New World Now Revealed: Hernán Cortés and the Presentation
  of Mexico to Europe', *Word and Image*, XXVII/1 (2011), pp. 31–46
Burkhart, Louise M., *Aztecs on Stage: Religious Theater in Colonial Mexico*
  (Norman, OK, 2011)
Carrasco, Davíd, 'Imagining a Place for Aztlan', in *The Aztec World*,
  ed. E. M. Brumfiel and G. M. Feinman (New York, 2008), pp. 225–40
Códice Chimalpopoca, trans. Feliciano Velázquez (Mexico City, 1975)
Coe, Sophie D., and Michael D. Coe, *The True History of Chocolate*
  (London, 1996)
Cortés, Hernando, *5 Letters of Cortés to the Emperor*, ed. J. Bayard Morris
  (New York, 1928)
Díaz del Castillo, Bernal, *The History of the Conquest of New Spain*, ed.
  D. Carrasco (Albuquerque, NM, 2008)

Dominici, Davide, Constanza Miliani and Antonio Sgamellotti, 'Cultural and Historical Implications of Non-destructive Analyses on Mesoamerican Codices in the Bodleian Libraries', in *Mesoamerican Manuscripts: New Scientific Approaches and Interpretations*, ed. M.E.R.G.N. Jansen, V. M. Lladó-Buisán and L. Snijders (Leiden, 2019), pp. 160–74

Durán, Diego, *Book of the Gods and Rites and the Ancient Calendar*, ed. and trans. F. Horcasitas and D. Heyden (Norman, OK, 1971)

—, *The History of the Indies of New Spain*, trans. D. Heyden (Norman, OK, 1994)

Feest, Christian, 'Mexican Featherwork in Austrian Habsburg Collections', in *Images Take Flight*, ed. A. Russo, G. Wolf and D. Fane (Florence, 2015), pp. 290–97

Filloy Nadal, Laura, and María Olvido Moreno Guzmán, 'Precious Feathers and Fancy Fifteenth-century Feathered Shields', in *Rethinking the Aztec Economy*, ed. D. L. Nichols, F. F. Berdan and M. E. Smith (Tucson, AZ, 2017), pp. 156–94

Fuentes, Patricia de, *The Conquistadors* (Norman, OK, 1963)

Gibson, Charles, *The Aztecs under Spanish Rule* (Stanford, CA, 1964)

Haag, Sabine, Alfonso de Maria y Campos, Lilia Rivero Weber and Christian Feest, eds, *El penacho del México Antiguo* (Altenstadt, 2012)

Hajovsky, Patrick Thomas, 'André Thevet's 'True' Portrait of Moctezuma and Its European Legacy', *Word and Image*, XXV/4 (2009), pp. 335–52

Hicks, Frederic, 'Ethnicity', in *The Oxford Encyclopedia of Mesoamerican Cultures*, ed. D. Carrasco (Oxford, 2001), vol. I, pp. 388–92

Hosler, Dorothy, 'Metal Production', in *The Postclassic Mesoamerican World*, ed. M. E. Smith and F. F. Berdan (Salt Lake City, UT, 2003), pp. 159–71

Keen, Benjamin, *The Aztec Image in Western Thought* (New Brunswick, NJ, 1971)

Landa, Diego de, *Relación de las Cosas de Yucatan*, ed. A. M. Tozzer (Cambridge, MA, 1941)

León-Portilla, Miguel, *Aztec Thought and Culture* (Norman, OK, 1963)

Lewis, Oscar, *Life in a Mexican Village* (Urbana, IL, 1963)

Lockhart, James, *The Nahuas after the Conquest: A Social and Cultural History of the Indians of Central Mexico* (Stanford, CA, 1992)

López Austin, Alfredo, and Leonardo López Luján, 'The Posthumous History of the Tizoc Stone', in *Fanning the Sacred Flame*, ed. M. A. Boxt and B. D. Dillon (Louisville, CO, 2012), pp. 439–60

López Luján, Leonardo, 'The Codex Mendoza and the Archaeology of Tenochtitlan', in *Mesoamerican Manuscripts*, ed. M.E.R.G.N. Jansen, V. M. Lladó-Buisán and L. Snijders (Leiden, 2019), pp. 15–44

—, *The Offerings of the Templo Mayor of Tenochtitlan*, trans. B. O. de Montellano and T. O. de Montellano (Albuquerque, NM, 2005)

Martyr D'Anghera, Peter, *De Orbe Novo: The Eight Decades of Peter Martyr*, trans. F. A. MacNutt, 2 vols (New York, 1912)

Motolinía [Fray Toribio de Benavente], *Memoriales o libro de las cosas de la Nueva España y de los naturales de ella*, ed. E. O'Gorman (Mexico City, 1971)

—, *Motolinía's History of the Indians of New Spain*, ed. and trans. E. A. Foster (New York, 1950)

Mundy, Barbara, 'Mapping the Aztec Capital: The 1524 Nuremberg Map of Tenochtitlan, Its Sources and Meaning', *Imago Mundi*, 50 (1998), pp. 11–33

Nichols, Deborah L., 'The Rural and Urban Landscapes of the Aztec State', in *Mesoamerican Archaeology: Theory and Practice*, ed. J. Hendon and R. Joyce (Oxford, 2004), pp. 265–95

Nicholson, H. B., 'The Annual "Royal Ceremony" on Mt. Tlaloc: Mountain Fertility Ritualism in the Late Pre-Hispanic Basin of Mexico', in *Mesas and Cosmologies in Mesoamerica*, ed. D. Sharon (San Diego, CA, 2003), pp. 33–49

—, 'Religion in Pre-Hispanic Central Mexico', in *Handbook of Middle American Indians*, ed. G. Eckholm and I. Bernal (Austin, TX, 1971), vol. X, pp. 395–446

Olivier, Guilhem, *Mockeries and Metamorphoses of an Aztec God: Tezcatlipoca, 'Lord of the Smoking Mirror'* (Boulder, CO, 2003)

Ortiz de Montellano, Bernard R., *Aztec Medicine, Health, and Nutrition* (New Brunswick, NJ, 1990)

Oudijk, Michel R., and Matthew Restall, 'Mesoamerican Conquistadors in the Sixteenth Century', in *Indian Conquistadors*, ed. L. E. Matthew and M. R. Oudijk (Norman, OK, 2007), pp. 28–63

Parsons, Jeffrey R., 'The Pastoral Niche in Pre-Hispanic Mesoamerica', in *Pre-Columbian Foodways*, ed. J. E. Staller and M. Carrasco (New York, 2010), pp. 109–36

—, and Mary H. Parsons, *Maguey Utilization in Highland Central Mexico* (Ann Arbor, MI, 1990)

Pasztory, Esther, *Aztec Art* (New York, 1983)

Place, Edwin B., and Herbert C. Behm, *Amadis of Gaul, Books I and II: A Novel of Chivalry of the 14th Century Presumably First Written in Spanish* (Lexington, KY, 2003)

Restall, Matthew, *Seven Myths of the Spanish Conquest* (Oxford, 2003)

—, *When Montezuma Met Cortés* (New York, 2018)

Riedler, Renée, 'Materials and Technique of the Feather Shield Preserved in Vienna', in *Images Take Flight*, ed. A. Russo, G. Wolf and D. Fane (Florence, 2015), pp. 330–41

Román Berrelleza, Juan Alberto, 'Health and Disease among the Aztecs', in *The Aztec World*, ed. E. M. Brumfiel and G. M. Feinman (New York, 2008), pp. 53–65

Sahagún, Bernardino de, *Florentine Codex: General History of the Things of New Spain*, ed. and trans. A.J.O. Anderson and C. E. Dibble, 12 vols (Salt Lake City, UT, 1950–82)

Sandstrom, Alan R., 'The Aztecs and their Descendants in the Contemporary World', in *The Oxford Handbook of the Aztecs*, ed. D. L. Nichols and E. Rodríguez-Alegría (Oxford, 2017), pp. 707–20

—, *Corn Is Our Blood* (Norman, OK, 1991)

Saville, Marshall H., *The Goldsmith's Art in Ancient Mexico* (New York, 1920)

Schroeder, Susan, 'Looking Back at the Conquest: Nahua Perceptions of Early Encounters from the Annals of Chimalpahin', in *Chipping Away on Earth*, ed. E. Quiñones Keber (Lancaster, CA, 1994), pp. 81–94

Tapia, Andrés de, 'The Chronicle of Andrés de Tapia', in *The Conquistadors*, ed. and trans. P. de Fuentes (Norman, OK, 1963), pp. 17–48

Tavárez, David, *The Invisible War: Indigenous Devotions, Discipline, and Dissent in Colonial Mexico* (Stanford, CA, 2011)

Thibodeau, Alyson M., et al., 'Was Aztec and Mixtec Turquoise Mined in the American Southwest?', *Science Advances*, 4/6 eaas9370, 13 June 2018

Thomas, Hugh, *Conquest: Montezuma, Cortés, and the Fall of Old Mexico* (New York, 1993)

Torquemada, Juan de, *Monarquía Indiana*, 3 vols (Mexico City, 1969)

Townsend, Camilla, *Fifth Sun: A New History of the Aztecs* (Oxford, 2019)

Townsend, Richard F., *The Aztecs* (London, 2000)

Umberger, Emily, 'Antiques, Revivals, and References to the Past in Aztec Art', *RES*, 13 (1987), pp. 62–105

—, 'Ethnicity and Other Identities in the Sculptures of Tenochtitlan', in *Ethnic Identity in Nahua Mesoamerica*, ed. F. F. Berdan et al. (Salt Lake City, UT, 2008), pp. 64–104

—, 'Tezcatlipoca and Huitzilopochtli: Political Dimensions of Aztec Deities', in *Tezcatlipoca: Trickster and Supreme Deity*, ed. E. Baquedano (Boulder, CO, 2014), pp. 83–112

Young, Allen, *The Chocolate Tree: A Natural History of Cacao* (Gainsville, FL, 2007)

ACKNOWLEDGEMENTS

Every book has its own genesis, life history and actors. This book is no exception, and I would like to take this opportunity to recognize the special contributions of the major actors that brought it to fruition. I would like first of all to express my thanks to Dave Watkins, Commissioning Editor of Reaktion Books, for suggesting I write this book, and for supporting, advising and encouraging me along the way. I also appreciate his perceptive editing. I am grateful to Alex Ciobanu, Assistant to the Publisher at Reaktion Books, for sharing his expertise on the sourcing of illustrations. Amy Salter, Editor at Reaktion Books, provided a smooth and efficient editorial experience, for which I am grateful. My thanks also go to Margaret McCormack for taking on the task of producing the Index. Jan Gasco and Mike Smith provided unique, essential illustrations; their collegiality is always greatly appreciated. Emily Umberger has been, as always, a most generous colleague in sharing her excellent detailed drawings. I would like to make particular note of the contributions of my daughter, Jennifer Berdan Lozano, for producing the maps and diagrams, for managing the images, and for her valiant efforts to bring me technologically into the twenty-first century. And a special note of gratitude goes to my husband, Bob, whose patience, wisdom and support are ever-present and ever-welcome.

▓▓ PHOTO ACKNOWLEDGEMENTS

The author and publishers wish to express their thanks to the below sources of illustrative material and/or permission to reproduce it. Some locations of artworks are also given below, in the interest of brevity:

Photos Frances F. Berdan: pp. 26, 39, 75, 82, 83, 97, 140, 186, 193 (right), 195, 200; from Frances F. Berdan and Patricia Rieff Anawalt, eds, *The Codex Mendoza*, vol. IV (Berkeley, CA, 1992): pp. 48, 91, 114, 119, 136; drawings Jennifer Berdan Lozano: pp. 12, 27, 42, 45, 56, 60, 65, 102, 128; Bodleian Libraries, University of Oxford (MS. Arch. Selden. A. 1): pp. 34, 64, 67, 106, 132, 133, 170; Brooklyn Museum, New York (CC BY 3.0): p. 10; Edward E. Ayer Digital Collection, Newberry Library, Chicago, IL: p. 23; Field Museum, Chicago, IL/photos Jennifer Berdan Lozano: pp. 81 (cat. no. 93835), 92 (cat. no. 164652); photo Janine Gasco: p. 90; The Metropolitan Museum of Art, New York: p. 175; courtesy Museo Nacional de Antropología, Mexico City: p. 53; National Museum of the American Indian, Smithsonian Institution, Washington, DC (cat. no. 108708)/photo Frances F. Berdan: p. 87; from Zelia Nuttall, ed., *The Book of the Life of the Ancient Mexicans, Containing an Account of their Rites and Superstitions*, or the *Codex Magliabechiano* (facsimile edn) (Berkeley, CA, 1903): pp. 149, 157, 167; courtesy Rhode Island School of Design (RISD) Museum, Providence, RI: p. 145; photo Patricia Rieff Anawalt: p. 193 (left); from Fray Bernardino de Sahagún, *Historia general de las cosas de nueva España*, or the *Florentine Codex* (1577), courtesy Biblioteca Medicea Laurenziana, Florence/World Digital Library: pp. 99 (book IX), 113 (book XI), 122 (book VIII), 126 (book X), 180 (book XII), 187 (book X); from Michael E. Smith, *The Aztecs*, 3rd edn (Chichester and Malden, MA, 2012), reproduced with permission: p. 118; from André Thevet, *Les vrais pourtraits et vies des hommes illustres grecz, latins et payens*, vol. III (Paris, 1584), photo courtesy Boston Public Library: p. 32; drawings Emily Umberger: pp. 30, 54, 161; Weltmuseum Wien/ KHM-Museumsverband, Vienna: pp. 72, 111.

Illustration page numbers are in *italics*